Andrew Thornton is an entrepreneur, speaker, author, advisor and coach to business leaders who see that businesses can be a force for good in society.

Along with his partner Eudora, he developed the heart way of doing business in his award-winning London supermarket, Thornton's Budgens. Together they founded Heart in Business, whose purpose is 'to uncover the Authentic Leader in us all, trusting that profit will follow'. He lives, writes, speaks and coaches the principles of Heart in Business on a daily basis.

He considers himself to be a 'visionary heart surgeon', having demonstrated that helping business leaders to open their hearts is the best way to build a sustainable and profitable business.

He was the co-founder of social enterprises The People's Supermarket and Food from the Sky, and founder of the consultancy SRCG. Prior to that, he worked at Ogilvy & Mather and Mars.

Holding a master's degree in Marketing from University College Dublin, Andrew splits his time between London and the Allgäu region of South Germany. He has two sons and a daughter. He loves to ski, run, swim, and cook and eat great food!

Eudora Pascall is a coach and facilitator to business leaders and an author writing on a more heartful approach to business. She has spent the last 20 years developing and growing the Heart in Business tools, techniques and methodology, influenced by teachings, study and experience across the world. Her purpose is that 'I unknot knots to bring direction, flow and purpose to your life by uncovering your gold together.' She passionately cares about helping people be the best of themselves.

Having studied at university in Britain, Germany and France, Eudora has several degrees, including a master's in organisational and individual change, cultural behaviour and economics. She is qualified professionally in transactional analysis as well as other individual psychological growth programmes, including COR in the UK and the US. Eudora has a unique, global background in the private, public and NGO sectors in Britain, Germany and France.

Eudora lives between Germany and London with her partner and daughter. She enjoys swimming, knitting and discovering more about different cultures.

Andrew's heart-centred ethos has practical application for large and small enterprises. This book demonstrates how being heart centred can deliver benefits for colleagues, customers and the planet.
– Charles Wilson, former CEO, Booker

Andrew's journey to a heart-centred business approach has lessons for all business leaders looking to create long-term value for all stakeholders – the 'why' question cannot just be profit anymore.
– Roger Whiteside, CEO, Greggs

The heart approach put forward in this book gives you a framework for developing your culture and fully engaging your people around your purpose. A framework that has a proven track record of success at Thornton's Budgens - bringing purpose to a business in a way that is so hard to achieve.
– Vittoria Varalli, VP National Wholesale, Sobeys

Putting the Heart Back into Business *is a must read for any conscious leader who believes that people are the key to a thriving business. It gives you proven tools to engage with all of your stakeholders so you can develop a more collaborative culture – as a B Corp, that's music to my ears.*
– Jayn Sterland, Managing Director, Weleda UK

This is a must-read book for anyone who believes business can be a force for good in society and still make a decent profit. So many of the broken aspects of the current business model are addressed by the heart approach put forward in this book; the full engagement of people is the only way forward!
– Professor Damien McLoughlin, Smurfit Business School, University College Dublin

In telling his own story of the journey from a head- to heart-centred business, Andrew brilliantly captures in a straightforward and practical way what I believe to be the key question for business leaders today. What kind of leader will you choose to be to address the pressing and unique problems that we face in the 21st century?
– Justin King CBE, former CEO, Sainsbury's

Growing a business for the long term, through good times and tough times, to the benefit of all stakeholders means nurturing the soul and working on its health. Andrew and Eudora have used their experience to set out some great insights and tools to help those responsible for taking their business on this journey. I'll certainly be encouraging my kids to read this as they develop their careers.
– Chris Martin, former CEO, Musgrave; NED, Wilko and ABP Food
   Group

I've been fortunate to know Andrew for 20 years and have long admired his spirit, passion and need for more. After reading his book I now know him a lot better and recognise where his 'need for more' came from. His book is a testimony to the power of belief: belief in people, belief that we can do better, and a belief that each of us has a role to play. It is typical of Andrew that rather than keep this 'secret' to himself, his instinct is to share, to get the word out. Passionate, heartfelt, honest – this is a book for our confusing times.
– Andrew Phipps, EMEA Head of Business Development and
   Global Futurist, Cushman & Wakefield

When the pressure comes to achieve performance targets and financial aims, there is a tendency for business leaders to revert to type, especially if colleagues seek to avoid the stark reality, and this can lead to unconstructive and disruptive behaviour. In this book Andrew and Eudora offer practical tools in order to identify and choose a more collaborative and productive way of being, enabling all stakeholders to face the harsh reality of their situation but at the same time work well together to resolve the challenges they face.
– Paul Monk, Executive Chairman, Compleat Food Group

As the world changes so radically around us, it is vital to understand the role you want to play and how that complements the people and organisations you work with. Putting the Heart Back into Business *provides the framework and multiple tools for every leader to navigate through the endless challenges of life. The book connects us with our inner core and guides us towards our own unique life, a life led with heart, and a business led with real purpose. By doing this work, we can make sense of the many challenges we experience in life and find ways to overcome the obstacles. But most of all, we can find a way to live the life we need and want every day, a life that is not just connected to ourselves but connected with everyone and everything around us – the way life is meant to be lived. I hope you will find this book as meaningful and liberating as I did.*
 – JP Donnelly, Country Manager, WPP

In this highly readable, compassionate and timely book, Andrew and Eudora succinctly capture the benefits that accrue to businesses by moving beyond the pure-profit motive to something more worthwhile. Laying out a series of logical and clearly explained templates for action, the book demonstrates how implementing such a transformation, whilst hard, is not impossible if you cleave to a meaningful and fulfilling purpose – no 'faking it to make it' – which then consistently informs attitudes and behaviours, allied to the concept of 'self-leadership'. In taking us through the remarkable journey they spearheaded at Thornton's Budgens, interspersed with fascinating interviews with employees and other business leaders who have embraced similar approaches, they not only deliver important guidance for business but also wise help on how to lead a better more, fulfilling life. Everybody will get something from this book.
 – Damian Thornton, Chairman, Stamford Partners

Putting the Heart Back into Business

PUTTING THE
Heart
BACK
INTO
BUSINESS

ANDREW THORNTON
& EUDORA PASCALL

Putting the Heart Back into Business
ISBN 978-1-912300-54-9
eISBN 978-1-912300-55-6

Published in 2022 by SRA Books
Printed in the UK

Ikigai illustration by Isobel Bast
Photographs by Chris Roche

The right of Andrew Thornton and Eudora Pascall to be identified as the authors of this work has been asserted in accordance with the Copyright, Designs and Patents Act 1988.

A CIP record of this book is available from the British Library.

Contents

To Hanne, James and Rory.

Foreword

Rita Clifton CBE

I heard about Andrew Thornton, the co-author of this book (with Eudora Pascall), well before I actually met him. I was doing some work with The Musgrave Group (which owned the Budgens brand from 2002 to 2015), and I kept on hearing about this extraordinary man who owned the most interesting and progressive stores within the Budgens franchise. From what I could glean, he was actually already doing so much of what many other grocery retailers were aspiring to do: real engagement with the local community, an imaginative and sincere approach to sustainability (with the 'Food from the Sky' initiative and others), and a very enlightened approach to developing his teams and employees. Having worked in sustainability and culture change for many years myself, I was very keen to meet him.

And so I did, and our conversations over the years have extended and deepened. I am thrilled that Andrew has written this book with Eudora, and opened his heart, business practices and personal as well as professional learnings over time. He is an example of the very human type of business leader that we – and business more generally – need as a positive exemplar of what good business can really do. For each other, for communities and for society more broadly.

I was also delighted to meet Andrew's co-author Eudora Pascall, and I know she has been instrumental in bringing to life the 'heart' vision at Thornton's Budgens through her coaching approach. Her approach to unknotting what stops people living a fulfilling life has been key to delivering change in the examples shared in the book. And Eudora's perspective beautifully complements Andrew's innovation. It's certainly a book about business with a real difference.

I know I am not alone in worrying that business as a whole can struggle with its perception as a positive force. It's slightly depressing that politicians often feel they get more votes from giving business a good kicking than supporting it. And yet, as we know, if we don't have good businesses delivering the products and services we need and paying appropriate taxes, we won't have the money or resources for schools, hospitals and civil society. Business needs public and political support to ensure effective freedom to operate.

It doesn't help that businesses and business leaders have often presented as an 'alien nation' – speaking in jargon, sometimes wearing stiff corporate uniforms and paying themselves in a way that can be truly out of this world. Not exactly helpful for building empathy and support for market economies, and not likely to build the kind of understanding and long-term relationships on which sustainably successful businesses depend. This is all magnified by a digital world where every action and word inside a business is now visible, and every misdeed is amplified with a scale and speed that can take your breath away. Whatever happens on the inside will get to the outside… so we all need to ensure that internal organisational reality is as good as we would like to say it is.

It's crucial that businesses act, and are seen to act, in a human way, for all their stakeholders, and that means business leaders need to behave and lead businesses in an authentically human way – as human beings who care about people, their families, communities and the planet. This is not incompatible with financially successful businesses – increasingly it is unacceptably high risk not to act well, as well as a wasted opportunity for sustainable growth. Numerous studies now highlight how (truly) purpose-led businesses outperform markets.

All this is why this excellent book by Andrew and Eudora is so important and helpful. Andrew brings his business head, human heart and deep practical experience to encourage and enable people to bring their best human selves to work and to lead. He and Eudora also bring so many vivid examples, practical tools and uplifting personal development thinking to help the reader. As a fellow personal development enthusiast myself, I know how valuable and transformational some of this work can be for individuals and organisations more broadly. It's also been gratifying to see that more and more business leaders have been prepared to share their personal stories and even vulnerabilities to help others with issues like mental health and resilience. Perhaps the most affecting elements of the book, however, are the personal stories and interviews with many of Andrew's very diverse employees; many have clearly had their working and personal lives transformed by his leadership, humanity and imaginative programmes.

To develop the kind of world we need, we need good businesses. Good businesses now and in the future need to have much more human leaders, acting in a way that reflects that humanity. We all need to ask ourselves what we can do to create the world we want. 'Heart in Business' is a fabulous contribution to how we can all ensure that happens.

Rita Clifton CBE has been called a 'brand guru' by the *Financial Times* and 'the doyenne of branding' by *Campaign* magazine. Alongside her board-chairing and non-executive roles, she is an author, columnist, keynote speaker, conference chair and practitioner on all aspects of brands, branding and business leadership.

Rita passionately believes in making

the world a better place and the role business has in this: 'I want to make business more human on every level – caring about the planet, about people, about helping society move forward. A big part of making businesses more human is making sure we have more diverse leadership and a much better gender balance running organisations. I love helping leaders realise their people will be happier, their customers will feel warmer towards them, and they'll create a lower-risk, higher-return business if they take a longer-term view.'

Rita's career has included being Vice Chair at Saatchi & Saatchi, London CEO and Chair of Interbrand and co-founder of BrandCap. She is now a portfolio chair and non-executive director on the board of businesses including John Lewis Partnership, Nationwide Building Society and Ascential plc. Her non-profit boards have included WWF (Worldwide Fund for Nature), the UK Sustainable Development Commission and Green Alliance. She was recently appointed Chair at Forum for the Future.

Introduction

Eight years ago, I realised I'd been seeking an alternative way of running a business – one that's heart centred rather than head centred; and one that's purpose centred rather than profit centred. As a result, I decided to write this book.

I had two false starts, but I believe it's no coincidence that it has been published now – at a time when society and businesses face the most challenging period many of us have lived through. As I write, we are emerging from the Covid pandemic, and we're facing an escalating climate crisis. There isn't a single business on the planet that can afford to avoid it – especially after the August 2021 report from the UN's Intergovernmental Panel on Climate Change (IPCC), which announced a 'code red for humanity'.

The climate crisis cannot be addressed without a lead from governments across the globe, but businesses have a crucial role to play too. There are two approaches business leaders can take. We can either wait and see what the government mandates us to do, or be on the front foot and act now, giving our businesses a big competitive advantage. And while this book is not about the climate crisis, I believe that if businesses embraced the heart-centred approach, it would transform how we deal with this huge challenge and dramatically speed up progress.

In parallel with this, there remains unprecedented inequality in the world and discrimination on the basis of wealth, sex, ethnic origin and sexual orientation. As I explore in Chapter 4, being the owner of a supermarket that employs people from many different races and cultures gave me a unique insight into the contribution all humans can make to a thriving business. It also highlighted the opportunities missed by business leaders who fail to recognise the potential in such diversity.

This book addresses a fundamental question – what is the role of business? Is it purely about making as much money as possible, or does business have a broader role to play in society? I believe it's the historic predominance of the former that has resulted in the climate and inequality crises. Over the past few decades, many businesses have become obsessed with profits, with that focus becoming ever more short term. A poor quarter's earnings can send a share price spiralling downwards, regardless of the long-term prospects of the business. And while I'm heartened that the importance of purpose in business is growing, I'm also concerned that it faces an uphill battle. As I write in October 2021, for example, Morrisons (the UK's fourth-largest grocer) has agreed a private equity sale, the nature of which encourages asset-stripping and profiteering.

This book puts forward an alternative perspective, one in which purpose sits at the centre of a business. That purpose can then become a force for good in the world. I believe that a heart-based alternative to the profit-focused approach can engage with all stakeholders in a way that leads to win–win situations where all of those stakeholders – and not just the shareholders – have a place at the table.

So, what's wrong with being a profit-centred business?

Most businesses will not end up in such extreme circumstances as Tesco did in the mid-2010s (more about that in Chapter 5), but being purely profit driven has an impact at numerous levels:

- ❤ **Leaders:** As a business leader, do you think that profit maximisation alone will help you live a fulfilling life? There's only so much money you can spend in your lifetime, so surely there must be more to aim for than this?

- ❤ **Employees:** Chasing profits provides even less satisfaction to employees than it does to its leaders. Many employees want to make a difference in the world, and a business with a meaningful purpose makes that possible. Millennial and Gen Z employees are far more discerning about who they work for than previous generations, posing a long-term existential threat to profit-centred businesses.

- ❤ **Customers:** There's no doubt that the 'profit at all costs' approach leads to environmental degradation, and the reward mechanism of this approach further increases inequality. Consumers are becoming more and more aware of this, and more discerning about how they spend their cash.

- ❤ **Environment:** Most businesses have now woken up to the climate crisis and started to recognise it's their responsibility to help deal with it. However, until environmental resources are properly priced through legislation, a focus on short-term profits will always lead to exploitation of those resources.

- ❤ **Engagement:** A 142-country study of 180 million employees by Gallup (see Resources) in 2013 found that only 13 per cent of people were engaged at work. That's a shocking statistic. They found that 24 per cent – almost a quarter of all respondents – were actively disengaged. That's not a good result for the business community. I know from experience that the heart-based approach engages way more than 13 per cent of employees.

And while I believe that heart-centred businesses are key to resolving the climate and inequality crises, I don't for one second believe that profit is a dirty word. Businesses need to generate a profit to survive, but when is enough, enough? My view is that businesses can make a decent profit *and* have a positive impact. Does the heart-based approach to business maximise profits? In the short term, probably not. In the long term, maybe – but does this matter? Is it the priority? Surely a decent return and a great contribution to society are what we should be aiming for?

Heart-centred businesses are fun to work for

My hypothesis is that open-hearted businesses are much more fun to work for, have a much longer sustainable future ahead of them, and are much more humane in their interactions with stakeholders. As I see it, this makes good business sense – take care of those who matter, and they will take care of you. And while more and more companies are embracing the need for purpose and the idea of responsible business, I also know that this approach will not land comfortably with everyone. However, if you've gone to the trouble of buying a book about putting the heart back into business, you've passed through the first gate.

If you're a business leader who is touched by the heart-centred way of being, you can start to change your business right away. There's no time like the present to begin to open your heart, and this book provides plenty of tools to help you do this. If you aren't sufficiently senior in your organisation or feel your perspective won't be heard, I can assure you there are plenty of open-hearted, purposeful businesses out there where you'd probably be a lot happier.

The idea is not a new one. That's why the title of this book refers to putting the heart *back* into business. Many of the original Quaker businesses had a heart – after all, it was Joseph Rowntree who invented the idea of the pension and the staff canteen. He considered that well-housed and well-fed workers were worth investing in – and saw that this was good business.

Why me?

I believe I'm well qualified to write this book because I've made this journey myself. My early working life was very much that of a profit-focused entrepreneur, but now I'm more than 10 years into my journey towards being an open-hearted leader. I say on a journey, as I think it's my life's work – and I doubt many people can say their heart is fully open all of the time. While this is largely my story and what I've learnt about opening my heart in a personal and business context, I've also interviewed a number of business leaders whom I respect, and their voices will be heard throughout the book. It feels as if everything I've done in my life so far has been preparing me for this time and for sharing the heart-centred approach.

Why us?

For most of the past eight years, I've been working on this book on my own. However, early in 2021, my partner Eudora challenged me on the fact that I'm yet another white, middle-class, privileged male author. Ouch! And a fair point, so I asked Eudora to collaborate with me. She is the co-founder of Heart in Business and we have worked together developing most of the content you will read here. She has also interviewed key team members at Thornton's Budgens, which will appear throughout the book. I believe that if you take the energy of these interviews and multiply it times the 60-odd people who work at Thornton's Budgens, it equals the impact of a business with a heart.

We have deliberately not referenced academic studies to back up our theories, but we will share how various tools and techniques have worked for us and other business leaders we know. We've linked together disparate bodies of work into one central approach that we call Authentic Leadership. And while I will put forward financial information from my own business and other case studies, I'm not going to present a fully researched financial case for open-hearted business, as this has been done well elsewhere (one great example is *The Heart of Business*, by Hubert Joly). And to be absolutely clear, when I use 'I' in this book, I'm referring to my personal experiences; when I use 'we', it refers to the heart-based work that Eudora and I have developed together.

Reasons to be optimistic

The signs are already everywhere, but I'll focus on the area I know best – the retail sector. Under its Project Earth plan, in summer 2020, London department store Selfridges launched a number of initiatives, including selling second-hand clothes, opening a repair service and renting furniture. I understand from a colleague who has helped them with customer research that this plan has been carefully developed. They have been tracking their customers for a number of years and now feel they're ready for these changes. Meanwhile, the Central England Co-op (which operates around 450 stores) is putting bike repair stations and toilets in all its stores (even the smaller ones). As its inspiring CEO Debbie Robinson told me: 'One of the things that stops people cycling to towns and villages to shop in different places is the lack of toilets.' A far-sighted retailer if ever there was one. Whatever happens next, I believe a heart-centred approach has to be a better way to do business. And maybe, just maybe, we can get off the hamster wheel and slow down a bit. Less commuting, more time with family and more time to reflect on what's important in life will all help us move forward in a more sustainable way.

How to approach this book

I believe you'll instinctively know when to tackle different aspects of this book. If you feel drawn to a particular section, then that's your starting point. We'll be sharing a number of exercises throughout the book, so I'd suggest buying a journal or notebook specifically for this purpose. Look out for the words 'YOUR TURN' and pause to complete the exercise that follows.

Have you ever attended a workshop where you planned to make changes but promptly forgot about them? One way to avoid this happening is to find yourself an accountability buddy. This could be a work colleague, your partner or a friend. You could work through the book together, or ask someone to hold you accountable for a specific change you want to make. At all times, trust your intuition.

I've spent most of my life working in the food business, so it's hardly surprising that many of the examples in this book come from that sector. However, I believe that the principles apply universally regardless of the sector, and are just as applicable to anywhere a group of people get together to achieve something. Eudora and I have also applied our principles to other areas including the charity, advertising, entertainment and IT sectors.

Beginnings

In order for you to understand how and why we evolved the heart-based approach, it's important for us to share our stories so far. I was born in Stockton-on-Tees, in the north of England, but when I was four weeks old my family returned to Ireland. So, even though I was born in the UK and have spent more than 35 years living there, I spent my formative years in Ireland and consider myself to be Irish. Because of my father's job, we moved around a lot – from England to Carlow (a few hours south of Dublin), and to Dublin. We then spent two years in Amsterdam before returning to Dublin. I'm deeply grateful to my parents for these moves, especially the two years we spent in Holland, which helped me develop an international view. As a student, I worked in the US; my first job took me to Wales and then England; my working life has always involved travel to and work in many different countries and now I split my time between London and Germany. I truly feel like a citizen of the world.

As my siblings will attest, I showed early promise as an entrepreneur. Some of my early schemes included selling Christmas trees and collecting old newspapers to sell for recycling. At the age of 12, I started my first paid job in Keogh's, our local newsagent. It was an early version of what would now be called a convenience store. Thanks to its owner, Declan O'Dowd, I caught the retail bug that remains with me to this day. Keogh's was literally underneath the head office of Superquinn, the iconic Irish food retailer founded by the late Feargal Quinn. Feargal remains a global food industry legend, and Declan was one of his up-and-coming managers who branched out on his own. I ended up working for Declan until my final year at university, in the latter days running the store for him at weekends and while he was on holiday.

When I graduated with a master's degree in marketing from University College Dublin, I was well prepared for my interviews and 48-hour selection panel with the confectionery company Mars – because I already knew a thing or two about selling sweets! They sent me to the UK for two years' training. Mars, based in Slough, just outside London, was an amazing place to work in the mid-Eighties. My peers went on to lead retailers such as Asda, Sainsbury's, Argos, Boots, the Post Office, Welcome Break, Loblaws and the Co-op, to name but a few. It really was a values-led business. Mars has five core principles – freedom, mutuality, efficiency, quality and responsibility – and we lived by them every day. The idea that a company could have its values written up in a glossy report and subsequently ignore them in its day-to-day operations was something I only discovered later in my working life. I also recognised the importance of bosses leading by example. Under the mutuality principle, there was a true sense of togetherness. Everyone at Mars clocked in – if the factory guys had to, then so did everyone else. The co-CEOs at that time were John and Forrest Mars, and they clocked in with the rest of us.

Just over three years later, I was headhunted by the advertising company Ogilvy & Mather and offered the chance to set up a new company within O&M's Research International division, replicating a consultancy business they had in the US. While I was loving every minute of working at Mars, the chance to create and run a business was too tempting. One year on, we hadn't made O&M a fortune and they'd been taken over by comms giant WPP. We were offered a management giveaway, which means we were paid off and given the company we'd started. It was a signal to go with the flow. Thus began my 16 years as CEO of the consultancy SRCG. We had many iterations over that time, with the latter five to six years focused back where I started, on strategic development in the convenience store and small-format retail sector. At our peak, we employed around 35 people and developed an excellent international reputation in our niche area. I loved the excitement of working in the US, many European countries, the Middle East and Asia, for such retailers and suppliers as Marks & Spencer, BP, Circle K, Spar, Musgrave, PepsiCo and Unilever.

Is that all there is?

In 2005 I found myself in the middle of a midlife crisis. I was married with two sons, then aged eight and ten; the founder and CEO of a successful consulting company; lived in central London; and had a lovely cottage by the sea. I recall sitting in my garden one sunny afternoon wondering, 'Is this it? Is this as good as it gets?'

A pivotal moment took place a while later over breakfast with my dear friend David in the Bailey Hotel in London. As we were about to say goodbye, he said: 'You are bored with your job – you need to do something different.' I kept playing those words over and over in my head, concluding that he was right – I did need a new challenge. I wasn't fulfilled or particularly enjoying myself. One of my biggest frustrations was about the meaningfulness (to me) of our consultancy work. That led to months of internal wrangling and discussions with my wife. Running the consultancy was more than a full-time job, so how could I create the space to figure out what to do next? Another breakthrough came over coffee a few months later.

I'd previously been part of a CEO mentoring organisation

called Vistage and stayed in touch with Coilin Heavey, who led our group, after I left. She helped me to see that, thanks to the success of the consultancy, I had enough equity in the properties I owned to remortgage and generate sufficient funds to live for two years without an income. My wife was very supportive and gave me the confidence to start the process of selling my share in the consultancy to my partners.

So, while other men going through a midlife crisis might buy a Porsche, I bought two supermarkets! My decision to quit SRCG and become a supermarket owner was driven by a desire to do something different. Looking back, I realise it was to create a revolutionary business model – one that was not all about short-term profits and that had some sort of meaningful purpose at its heart.

As we entered 2020, the pace of life seemed to be at breaking point. I did a lot of public speaking around the world, and often used the image of a hamster running faster and faster in its wheel to wonder whether there was a different way. No matter where I was in the world, when I asked 'Who is continuously exhausted and worn out?', I always saw plenty of raised hands. Then, as I was finishing this book, a university classmate died at the age of 58. He was the CEO of one of the Irish banks caught up in the 2008 financial crisis. The stress must surely have contributed to his untimely death. I certainly didn't have a grand plan at this stage, just a sense that I needed to move in a different direction. I resonate with what Steve Jobs once said – while at the time his moves were not always obvious, afterwards it was easy to look back and join the dots.

The early days of Thornton's Budgens

Looking back at my first few years of being a supermarket owner, it was all about community and the environment. While I was an industry consultant at SRCG, I regularly spoke at conferences about how easy it was to compete against the likes of Tesco (who had started to encroach on the convenience sector) by being a community retailer and doing things that a centrally managed, command-and-control business could not. Around that time, Musgrave (an Irish client of ours at SRCG) bought the long-established Budgens brand and were in the process of converting it into a franchise along the lines of SuperValu and Centra in Ireland. After an initial conversation with Martin Hyson (the Budgens director responsible for divestment) and months of discussions, Budgens agreed to sell me their store in the north London suburb of Crouch End.

I borrowed a stack of money and, in early October 2006, Thornton's Budgens was up and running. What followed was a baptism of fire. While I had experience of developing retail strategy, I had zero experience of running a store of this size. It turned over about £175,000 a week, employed around 80 people, and was way bigger and more complicated than Keogh's. It was run by a manager who did a good job under the command-and-control culture of a corporate Budgens, but struggled with my hands-off style.

It was a tough first year, but I slowly started to get a grip on the operational side. Less than six months after buying Crouch End, Martin Hyson agreed to let me buy a second store in nearby Belsize Park. There were certainly some hairy moments in the early days. Debora, one of the Crouch End managers, described me as an 'ideas factory'. And while being creative can be advantageous, when combined with a lack of a clear and well-defined purpose, it can lead to chaos. I was all over the place and my team, who were trained to do as the boss says, followed.

Despite all of that, in year two we won Independent Retailer of the Year at the prestigious Retail Industry Awards and started to win environmental awards. Surely we were on track? Despite my exhaustion, we did have some breakthrough ideas.

Here are the three I'm proudest of:

1. **Pennies for Plastic**

   In 2002, Ireland was one of the first countries to introduce a plastic bag charge, which reduced consumption by more than 90 per cent. It seemed an obvious idea, but the UK was slow to act. However, in 2007, we became the first UK supermarket to stop giving away free carrier bags. Together with Clare Richmond, a creative marketer and Crouch End local, we created Pennies for Plastic. The idea was simple – for every unused plastic bag, we gave the cost (1p) to a charitable fund. Over four years, across both stores, we collected and gave away £125,000 to more than 40 different local good causes (saving 1.25m carrier bags). For me this was a win–win scheme. I tried to recruit some of the major supermarkets to do the same, but failed this time round.

2. **Food from the Sky**

   I was fortunate enough to get to know the eco-chef Arthur Potts-Dawson and was impressed by the small herb and vegetable garden on the roof of his Acorn House restaurant in King's Cross. After that I met Azul Thome, who approached me about a local food-growing project. When I took her up to our empty 3,000 sq ft flat roof, her eyes lit up. Together we came up with the idea of turning it into a farm, which was run as a separate social enterprise. Locals who wanted to improve their connection with food helped us to run the garden, and we sold the output downstairs in the store – ploughing all the income back into the farm. It was beautiful and great fun.

3. **Chiller doors**

   A study allegedly carried out by Coca-Cola (I say allegedly as it was often discussed in the supermarket industry, but I never saw a copy – perhaps it was an urban myth) showed that doors on soft drinks chillers were a barrier to sales, and that sales were higher from chillers with no doors. This idea was taken on by supermarkets globally, so that by the early 21ˢᵗ century, most supermarkets used open chillers for most products. These chillers cost way more to run and burnt almost twice as much carbon, so we set out to prove that this received wisdom was a myth. By retrofitting doors on all our meat and dairy chillers, we proved that sales were not lost and chiller running costs could be cut by 46 per cent in the process. And while the CEO of one of the major UK chains said that their customers didn't like the idea, mine got it immediately and were very supportive. I subsequently discovered that the major chain had researched the idea in focus groups and encountered resistance. It seemed like a hassle, so why support it? When we did it, people understood the benefits and realised it wasn't a hassle to open the doors. Slowly but surely, 12 years on, more and more retailers are following our lead.

I should also mention the initiatives that didn't work – such as inviting a local nutritionist to speak to customers in our Crouch End store on a Saturday morning, or our zero-packaging section in Belsize Park. They were ideas ahead of their time. Another idea we experimented with was a series of recordings created by another Crouch End local to help people be more mindful and reflect on their emotions. It could've worked, but before it had any chance to bed in, I was on to the next idea and our focus drifted away.

Heartbreak... and then a slow death

During the second year of Thornton's Budgens, something else began to gnaw away at me – that it wasn't just my job that had become unfulfilling. My wife and I seemed to have drifted apart. We lacked common goals or even a direction. I knew deep inside my heart (even if I couldn't fully articulate it at the time) that I was being called to move in a different direction, and it wasn't one that had any appeal to my wife. Telling my sons that their parents were going to separate was the most difficult thing I've ever had to do. And while I generally don't have regrets, this is one conversation that I'd like to have a second go at.

Then, in 2008, an inevitable event happened in UK retail – Woolworths went bust. For me it was a life-changing moment, as there was a decent-sized Woolworths five doors up from my Crouch End store. There was already Thornton's Budgens, the Tesco Express next door, an M&S Simply Food, along with numerous independent convenience stores, fruit and veg shops, a butcher and an organic and health food store. In other words, plenty of food retail space. The moment I heard about Woolworths' demise, I knew another food retailer would be arriving on our doorstep. Despite getting out my old consultant's black book and contacting CEOs of various non-food retailers such as Argos and Poundland to try to engage their interest, my worst nightmare came true, and Waitrose took the site in the autumn of 2009. If I'd had a list of retailers I did *not* want to take the site, in order of priority it would have been Waitrose, Waitrose and Waitrose!

As a result, we experienced three years of slow death. After a healthy start (we only lost 18 per cent of our turnover in week one, versus a predicted 25–30 per cent), each week that passed saw Waitrose chipping away at our turnover. Our customers loved what we stood for, yet too many were tempted by the allure of Waitrose, even if just for the occasional basket. We lost money every week and, despite support from Musgrave, by the end of 2012 I was exhausted. I was putting everything I had into keeping the ship afloat and, despite the fact that Belsize Park was doing really well, everything we made there was lost in Crouch End. It was soul destroying.

Just before Christmas 2012, I had another defining meal with a friend. He asked me what I most wanted for 2013. My answer was twofold – to sort out Thornton's Budgens by finding a viable way forward and, having done that, to take a three-month sabbatical to refresh and regroup. And that's what I did. Thanks to the support of Budgens' regional director Gavin Claxton, who was my partner in what I described at the time as a conscious negotiation, we agreed a deal for Budgens to acquire the Crouch End store. I say a conscious negotiation because I broke all the rules about keeping my cards close to my chest. I shared exactly what I wanted. Gavin felt my needs were fair and reasonable and together we went about securing them. My lesson here was that there's no need to play a game; you can get what you want by putting your cards on the table.

Discovering my purpose

On 6 June 2013, I was on a plane to India for the first part of my three-month sabbatical. The day before that, I'd had yet another fateful meal – lunch with my friend Nicolas. He casually asked whether I intended to write a book about my 'somewhat unusual approach to running a business'. Having never thought about this before, the words 'Yes, it would be called *Putting the Heart Back into Business*' came out of my mouth. I hadn't even connected this book sitting inside me with the creative writing course I'd planned as the final part of my sabbatical.

So much happened in India, and the idea of the heart kept returning to me. I started to explore the idea of individuals having a purpose – the Indians call it *swadharma* (*swa* means own, and *dharma*, duty). It's their own 'unique role in life or way of being in the world, which it is their duty to realise and fulfil'. I realised that mine was all about putting the heart back into business, and that for Thornton's Budgens the missing (and most important) dimension was our people, followed by community and the environment. I also realised that the key to unlocking people was to open their hearts. I stretched myself by signing up for a three-day creative painting workshop at the Osho Ashram in Pune. Our teacher said: 'Just start painting, don't think or plan – just paint.'

I did, and a huge heart emerged that filled the wall-sized canvas. When I returned to Belsize Park, I realised it fitted exactly on one wall of the windowless space I used as an office/meeting room. It was meant to be there.

Another significant moment on my journey was meeting Azul, my co-founder at Food from the Sky, about a year after my marriage ended. We ended up being more than business partners; I moved to Crouch End, and we lived together on and off for five years. I didn't have a clue what this heart idea might look like or how it could be applied, so I spent a year reading, writing about and meeting CEOs to explore the idea of heart in business. As a result, I ran the first heart workshops with Azul at Thornton's Budgens in late 2013. By early 2015, I was ready to form an organisation and gathered together a small group I'd met on my personal development journey – all of whom I felt understood business, having worked in organisations themselves. Azul and I had parted by then, and that initial group included Eudora.

Over the past 11 years, I've explored numerous different approaches and they formed the basis for Heart in Business – where personal development meets business development. Our purpose is 'to uncover the Authentic Leader in us all, trusting that profit will follow' and our mission is 'to equip leaders to discover the purpose in everyone, to inspire the company to honour its reason for being, so that everyone can be in flow through unknotting and live at their full potential'.

We support businesses through this journey to the heart through a mix of coaching, training, facilitation and advisory support. We call what we do Accelerated Transformation Coaching (ATC) – it is our unique approach to uncovering the Authentic Leader in you and getting to the nub of what your purpose in life is. We focus on unknotting what is stopping you living a totally fulfilling life, as we believe that we are all leaders in different aspects of our lives, and that this unknotting process helps you access that leadership – it is a form of alchemy.

ATC is the thread that runs through all our work with business leaders and their teams. This proven method gets results that are rapid and long lasting, meaning your business can start to transform immediately and your people can quickly learn to develop productive and collaborative behaviours – this builds a more resilient and profitable business.

Our Stepping into Your Authentic Leadership series of training programmes is a key part of this process of helping people to open their hearts.

Eudora and I moved in together in 2015, and her daughter Hanne became my stepdaughter. Two years later, Hanne imploded at the German school in west London. Despite being only eight, she couldn't see how school was helping her grow. Her dyslexia was a factor in this, along with her free spirit. Together with her father, we decided to home-school her for a couple of years. With Eudora being half-German and the fact that Germany has a much more varied school system, we decided that Hanne would be better off going to school there (when she was ready). We split our time between the UK and Germany, with Eudora home-schooling Hanne in Germany and Hanne's father doing the same in London. And then, in September 2020, Hanne started attending a school in Lindau, in South Germany, which meant that she and Eudora had to move there, with me continuing to split my time between the two countries.

Just before the first UK lockdown in March 2020, I was diagnosed with adrenal fatigue (effectively a burnout) and was advised that if I didn't take some time off work, I would become very ill. Having been about to cancel our forthcoming trip to Germany to join the team at the store as pandemic panic-buying took hold, I did an about-turn and went to Germany. I didn't expect to be away until August, but as soon as I stopped working, my whole system crashed. I listened to my body and did what I needed to do to recover.

Saying goodbye to Belsize Park

That summer, I had an approach from one of the major chains. They'd been trying to buy the store in Belsize Park for years. And while I hadn't been at all interested up to that point, this time they seemed more serious, and I started to wonder whether it was time to move on. It was becoming more and more difficult for an independent one-store food retailer to survive in London – what with continuous rent and rates pressures, retail moving online and the continued growth of discounters. And maybe, just maybe, the pressure of keeping the show on the road was taking its toll and had contributed to my adrenal fatigue. I realised I needed to do something radically different with the store or recognise that it was time to sell.

The year 2021 was a bit of a rollercoaster ride, and while the intentions of the multiple that wanted to buy the store were good, I didn't want almost 15 years' worth of work to be washed away. January was a particularly tough month. While two independents were interested in the store, for various reasons their offers were not viable. However, I knew that a new chapter was calling me. I needed more freedom and time to dedicate to sharing the heart approach with other businesses – but while I still owned the store, would this book ever get written?

It was with a strange combination of reluctance and gratitude that I accepted the offer from the multiple. Then, out of the blue, Irish retailer the Kavanagh Group (whom I had known for years) approached with an interest in buying the store. They wanted to carry on a lot of what I'd created and were open to me being involved in how they developed the business. They recognised that I had skills that they did not, while I recognised there was a lot that they could bring to the store. After a process that took almost a year, the Kavanagh Group bought the Belsize Park store in June 2021.

When I announced I was selling, I was bowled over by the emails

I received from people in our industry as well as customers. I want to share the two messages that touched me the most because I think they demonstrate what you can achieve when you run an open-hearted business. The first was from James Perry, chairman of COOK ready meals: 'You really have almost single-handedly shifted the Overton window in terms of what is thought possible in the UK grocery industry. I hope you are able to take a step back and celebrate an extraordinary achievement with Thornton's Budgens, maybe even rest a bit before you charge on, as you inevitably will. Can't wait to watch you climb the next mountain. Huge respect.'

(The term 'Overton window' refers to the range of policies regarded as acceptable in a particular sphere, often specifically used in that of politics.)

The other was from the distinguished actor Dame Janet Suzman, who was a customer as well as a big fan: 'I'm really most sorry to hear this and yet at the same time really pleased that you're passing on your expertise. Jack Lemmon, I think it was, once said: "When the elevator reaches the top floor it has to be sent down again to pick up the others", which is what you're doing, and bravo. Your changes have been thrilling to watch and your fresh thinking a tonic. So few people think out of the box, and you have, and you do. I wish you a marvellous second chapter to a terrific life, Andrew. I'm proud to know you.'

Having made my decision to sell the store, various companies approached me to offer their support and new doors began to open. As I write, I'm entering into a new cycle with excitement and uncertainty. After 30-plus years of being a CEO, I'm looking forward to being an advisor and non-executive director (NED) to a number of different organisations and to be able to dedicate more time to our Heart in Business work. And I know the roles I take on in the future need to be with businesses that want to be more heart centred.

Eudora's story

I've described how I met Eudora, but it's essential to know that, in addition to being my partner in life as well as in Heart in Business, she has 15 years of experience in coaching CEOs, board members, couples, families and individuals. She has studied organisational and individual change, psychology, coaching, cultural behaviour and economics in three countries and has a master's in international studies and diplomacy. Eudora spent more than 20 years developing and growing her Dare to Rethink methodology (helping individuals to understand who they are and rethink who they want to be).

She was born in Bonn, Germany, but moved to South Wales when she was six – an experience that she found extremely challenging, not least because she was bullied for being different. She found solace in a thought-provoking education at a Quaker boarding school, where she was surrounded by international students. She explains: 'I went on to study and work in three countries – Britain, Germany and France. I've worked in the public, private, charity and education sectors in all three countries. I later did a master's degree in London. I've never stopped learning different coaching and facilitation methods as well as business, economics and languages.'

She has experienced a great deal of loss in her life (her father died when she was 25, then her mother, followed by several close relatives and friends), and became a single parent in her early 30s. What motivates her is a desire to share what she has learnt from her experiences and to support others through their challenges.

'I remember the moment I met Andrew,' she says. 'He opened the door to me at an event and I knew he was the one. He was wearing a purple velvet jacket and I was convinced he was an English professor from Scotland! It took me two years to realise he wasn't an English professor from Scotland, and it took Andrew two years to realise I was the one he wanted to make a life with. Andrew and I fit well together both at work and at home. I've always been passionate about encouraging businesses to be more heartful and assumed everyone else felt the same. Andrew has the same passion, and it's a delight to work and live with someone who shares this passion. It has become commonplace that my daughter, Andrew and I sit at the dinner table and discuss how being more connected to your feelings and more authentic in your communication, with a pinch of humour, can bring the necessary oil to any situation.'

A word about spirituality and trust

If you mention spirituality in a business context, it can often scare people. It comes into play for me because I believe we're all part of an interconnected system – we're not separate from animals, nature or the planet. It makes no difference whether you follow an organised religion or have your own spiritual practice; I believe we're all in this together and the actions I take have an impact on others, and that in turn comes back to impact me in some shape or form. This links to the concept of karma – defined (in Hinduism and Buddhism) as 'the sum of a person's actions in this and previous states of existence, viewed as deciding their fate in future existences' – i.e. what goes around comes around. My view is that there's a natural flow to life and if I'm open and aware of that, then I'll know what to do. I've learnt the hard way that if something seems like hard work on an ongoing basis, then something isn't working.

At the Crouch End store, we needed to take the fight to Waitrose and go deeper into what we stood for. There came a point when it felt like swimming upriver, and I realised I needed to let go and move on. At the time I was furious with Waitrose and their CEO Mark Price. I've subsequently got to know Mark and shared my deep gratitude with him because, if Waitrose hadn't opened a branch in Crouch End, I might still own two stores and wouldn't have had the time and space to develop Authentic Leadership or write this book. So now, when things are tough and not flowing, I do try to step back and trust – asking myself, what does this mean, what can I learn from this, how do I need to shift course? This not only helps me shift but also reduces the stress of swimming against the flow. I can be slow to reach the point of trust and letting go, but I'm getting better at it. With hindsight, in the case of Crouch End I probably held on for a year more than was ideal – at personal cost to my health and wellbeing.

Eudora sees it like this: 'Have you ever heard a song, read a sentence, heard a child laugh or looked at a sunrise and felt a shiver down your spine, felt yourself connect more deeply to yourself and the world in that moment? These are the experiences that remind us what's real and what's important. To trust is to be willing to be affected by something. Spirituality is to recognise a feeling or sense that there is something greater than yourself. I have seen the Thornton's Budgens team step into greater trust and connectedness, where differences melted away and the joint purpose brought them together. This was particularly visible during moments of stress, for example when there was an attempted armed robbery in the store, or at the beginning of the Covid pandemic – but it was also there in the everyday when customers could feel the trust and connectedness.'

This matter of interrelatedness and spirituality is highly personal and whether you are with me on this or not doesn't actually matter. Assume for a second that we're all independent and not connected. If I believed that, I'd still feel that allowing people to be their authentic selves would be a good thing and make businesses function more effectively.

♡ 2

Personal Purpose

I believe that purpose is fundamentally linked to living an open-hearted life, and that it applies both to individuals and organisations. I also believe that the first step in the journey to becoming a heart-centred leader is to identify your personal purpose. According to most dictionaries, purpose means: 'The reason for which something is done or created or for which something exists.' Many companies and individuals use the words mission or vision for what I would call purpose, but in my view the key is having an overriding purpose/mission/vision that drives everything you do.

There's no set formula to finding your purpose, and I accept that it's probably the most difficult thing we'll ask you to do in this book. I know that, in our workshops, this is usually the part that participants find the hardest, so don't beat yourself up if it doesn't come to you straight away. In an ideal world, finding your personal purpose would be the first step on the journey to becoming a heart-centred leader, but don't worry if it's not clear at the start. Work on other areas and trust that it will become clear to you when the time is right. For me, a purpose is a set of words that I can connect to, that mean something to me. So, I encourage you to do the exercises and write down some words that mean something to you, without worrying about the quality of the words or comparing them to someone else's. We've deliberately given you quite a few exercises in this chapter, so complete the ones that appeal to you and keep making notes as insights come to you.

My search for purpose stemmed from my midlife crisis, which was brought on by feeling a sense of incompleteness as well as the pain of going through a divorce and the break-up of my family. I kept asking myself, 'What's the point? Why do I work so hard yet still feel empty inside?' Since then, I've been searching for what's missing and do feel I'm getting closer to it. As part of the process, I've come to believe that we're all here on this planet at this time for a reason. I only realised this in my late 40s, and yet many people will die without ever having considered this or finding out what their purpose is.

A few years ago, I co-facilitated a life purpose workshop for a group of business leaders with my colleague, Ralph. When some of the group seemed a bit daunted by the task, Ralph used the words 'ways of being', which means how you choose to be in the world and live your life. For a number of people, the lights came on and this seemed less grand than finding a life purpose, so it might work for you too. In this context, ways of being are defined as: 'Reflecting what's going on for you internally [your mental and emotional state, your thoughts and how you feel in your body], and how you respond – what you think, say and do.'

The magic of *ikigai* and *Shantaram*

The Japanese have a word for life purpose – *ikigai,* which literally means 'a reason for being'. I have also heard it described as 'the reason I get up in the morning'.

Figure 1 shows how this works. It's really simple – if you find yourself in the sweet spot where the four circles intersect, then you're more likely to find yourself springing out of bed in the morning, full of joy! Let me use the example of my midlife crisis to illustrate this – with the proviso that I'm doing this with the benefit of hindsight, as I wasn't aware of this way of thinking at the time.

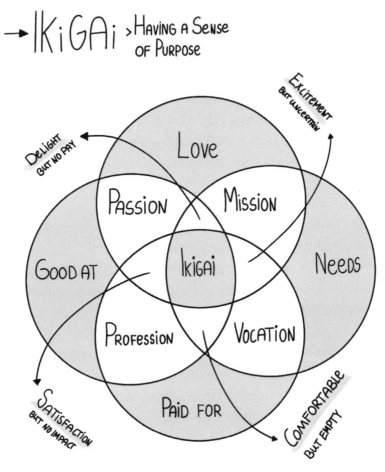

→ IkiGAi > Having a Sense of Purpose

Figure 1: Ikigai

At the consultancy, I was very good at what I did and, for 14 of the 16 years I was there, loved it. The last two years were harder, and that was probably connected to the third circle – 'Does the world need this?' I found myself getting more and more disillusioned with our clients' motivation for commissioning our work. Was it just a box-ticking exercise? Was it really going to make a difference in the world and to people's lives? (I must stress these were my feelings and no reflection on the quality of the work we did.) The final circle is 'What I can be paid for'. That certainly worked for me in the consultancy, where I mostly earned good money – in fact, a lot more than I have earned since – but even with a big pay cheque, it was not enough to compensate for the lack of fulfilment in the other circles. Looking at Figure 1, the phrase 'comfortable but empty' would have resonated with me while I sat in my garden by the sea all those years ago. Had I known about this model then, using it might have helped me become clearer about why I wasn't feeling fulfilled and give me some clues as to what I should do with my life.

> YOUR TURN: *Create a purpose section in your journal. Look at the ikigai model: how does your life pan out in each of the four circles? How do you feel when you do this? Do any of the comments on the chart resonate with you? Is there anything in your life that you need to change?*

Another perspective can be found in one of my all-time favourite books – *Shantaram*, by David Gregory Roberts, a former heroin addict and convicted bank robber who escaped from jail in Australia and fled to India. The main protagonist, Lin, operates various illegal activities as part of a gang, and the book is clearly somewhat autobiographical. The gang have their own spiritual guru, Idriss, and in the sequel, *The Mountain Shadow*, Idriss poses the question: 'What is the purpose of life?' In answer to his own question, he replies that the purpose of life is to 'express a positive set of characteristics'. When asked to define these positive characteristics, he says that they are found wherever people 'live humanely with one another'. In simple terms, the invitation is to identify your positive characteristics and live them as fully as you can. This caused me to consider what my positive characteristics might be. They include: the ability to open my heart; being a visionary and seeing things before others can; being a good storyteller; being able to connect the spiritual and business worlds; wanting to make a difference in the world. And while I was already clear on my purpose when I read Idriss's words, this list certainly fits well with it.

> YOUR TURN: *In the purpose section of your journal, write down your positive characteristics. Be generous and include everything that occurs to you (without editing it – no one but you will read this). Take your time – and keep coming back to this so you can add to the list.*

Eudora's insights into purpose

Eudora is familiar with the feelings of emptiness I've experienced on my journey. A lot of clients come to her because their lives lack meaning or direction. 'They say that they feel empty inside and are searching for something on the outside,' she explains. 'They feel unhappy and lost, and my job is to help them find or rediscover their life purpose.' She sees purpose as much more than a professional path: 'It's an overriding statement that speaks to and impacts all parts of your life, including how you show up at work, how you are with your family, your friends, yourself and even complete strangers. Purpose is your "why". It sums up what's behind who you are and what you do. It's the reason you get up in the morning and what keeps you going when you feel like giving up.' There is, she says, a subtle difference between mission, purpose and vision: 'Purpose keeps you focused on why you exist; it's the why behind the action. Vision is the ability to plan the future with imagination and aligns you with your purpose. Mission is how you will accomplish it, the action you need to take.'

Having a clear purpose helps you cut through the chaos and decide where to focus your energy. It can also strengthen your resolve and support you in achieving your dreams: 'We are all born with a purpose and some of us have the good fortune to stay connected to it from an early age,' says Eudora. 'Unfortunately, most of us forget or become disconnected from it because of other people's expectations. It can take many years to start listening to that small inner voice inviting us to rediscover and reconnect to our calling.

'Andrew and I had the good fortune to meet Bernardine Evaristo on the night she won the Booker Prize. We had read and loved her book *Girl, Woman, Other*, and when Andrew saw her before the announcement, he wished her luck and they hugged. She was open, humble and as excited as a schoolgirl. It took Bernardine 60 years to finally be recognised on the world stage for her body of work. Her latest book, *Manifesto*, is about never giving up. She says that there's a manifesto in each of us – a knitted patchwork of our life experiences, the generations that came before us, the struggles we've experienced and the hope for a better future for all. I see this manifesto as another way of describing personal purpose. I also believe that the less privileged in society have the greatest need for a personal purpose or manifesto. The more privileged you are, the less you need to fight to understand your drive and direction because so much is already available to you. Ironically, however, having it all can lead to an empty feeling inside. I continue to be moved by Bernardine and others who have used their experiences to fuel their desire for change. Do you dare to rethink and change?'

Finding your purpose

Step one in the process of finding your purpose is to acknowledge the need or desire for one. You also have to start clearing out old habits and ways of being to get clarity on your purpose. Most of the exercises in this book will help you clear out the old so you can welcome in the new. A crisis can provide the crunch point, something that leads you to question what life is all about. Time out from your normal routine can also help with the development process.

As magical things always happen when I go to India, my current purpose was refined on an eight-day walk with business leaders along the river Narmada – which was definitely time out of my normal routine. The current iteration of my purpose is as follows: 'I am a visionary heart surgeon: I help leaders heal so that they can help others shine. I am a student, a teacher and a storyteller.' As I'm all about putting the heart back into business, the implication here is that the heart is somehow blocked – hence the need for a heart surgeon. The need to help leaders heal so that they can help others shine will hopefully become clear to you as you read on. The last part comes from my desire to keep learning as well as teach – I believe that being on a continuous learning quest keeps me feeling alive and fresh. Finally, I wanted to acknowledge that, as an Irishman, I'm a natural storyteller and that storytelling is a powerful way to motivate people to look at things differently.

Eudora's purpose is rather beautiful: 'I unknot knots to bring direction, flow and purpose to your life by uncovering your gold together.' As a child she loved unknotting knots and remembers lying awake thinking about how she could best tackle a particular knot. This obsession was channelled into knitting, and she still loves the challenge of turning thousands of knots into a jumper, scarf or hat. She also found her childhood experiences confusing and often felt very knotted inside, not understanding the emotions she was experiencing. It was only as a young woman that she started to feel safe, loved and seen. Her knots started to fall away, and she began to understand the reasons why they were there.

'I assumed everyone knew their purpose and it was only later that I realised this is not the case,' she says. 'It was when my knots started to soften that I was able to be present and start focusing on my purpose and what I love doing. I know what it feels like to be so knotted inside that you are frozen in fear, sadness and anger, unable to move. I want to enable others to unknot themselves so that they can become clear on their flow and purpose and fill that hole inside. I feel an immense sense of delight, pride and achievement every time one of my clients' knots falls away. I enjoy watching the relief and realisation in their eyes as they understand that particular knot and why it's no longer serving them. They become lighter, stand taller in the world and start making purposeful strides forward. This is my desire for us all.'

Uncovering core wounds

Another important step in discovering your purpose is to identify and understand your core wounds. So, what exactly is a core wound? 'We all fall down and hurt ourselves many times in our lives,' says Eudora. 'We can pretend we never fell, but the scars will still be there to tell the tale. We need to process the emotions attached to an experience in order to move forward. If we don't, these unprocessed emotions will leak out when we least expect or want them to. This is the nature of a core wound.'

One of Eudora's core wounds was created when her father died. She says: 'I had no one to mourn with and felt very alone. For a long time, I wanted to stay in the pain and suffering because it was the only way I could stay connected to my father. Slowly, over time, I did go through the pain and found a new way of being, with my father in my heart.' As a result, she has found her strength, power and purpose. The painful experiences of her life have shaped who she is today and how she shows up as a friend, mother, partner, coach and sister. 'The way we respond to the pain and difficulty of our core wounds can connect us to our true calling,' she says.

> YOUR TURN: *In your journal, write down the things in your past that have wounded you and caused you great pain. Write about how they impacted you then and how they impact you now. This may be uncomfortable but stick with it.*

When I developed my purpose, I wasn't really thinking about my core wounds, but I can see some connections now. There's no doubt that I failed to shine in the Irish school system – I didn't get the chance to be in flow at school (other than during my two years in Holland) and my positive characteristics were deeply hidden – having had a taste of what this could be like in Holland made the rest of my school days in Ireland even more painful. Access to my creativity was shut down until I went to university, and with that, my heart closed too. This experience has helped me to focus on helping others to open their hearts, to always shine and be the best of themselves. And it also explains why I'm so keen to keep on learning. I think my storyteller emerged from the desire to get attention, and while this wasn't always the case, I think I am now using that particular wound to positive effect.

Finding your flow

You can also apply the concept of flow to the development of your personal purpose. Being 'in flow' means you're engaging in an activity that you love, and you become so absorbed in what you're doing that you lose track of time. You become one with that activity and everything around you. The concept has existed for hundreds of years, but it was Mihaly Csikszentmihalyi who popularised it. He observed musicians in an orchestra and asked the question: 'Why are they happy?' He found that they were doing what they loved, with a clear purpose, and concluded that happiness = purpose + flow. He talks about the juxtaposition between challenge and skill and how, if you find a balance between the two, you can get into your flow channel. However, if you are over-challenged and don't have the required skill, you may feel anxious. And if you engage in an activity that involves less skill, you may become bored. He also talks about an activity that you love growing from being pleasurable to a passion, and leading to your higher purpose. If we're encouraged to experience and live our purpose, we grow into the best of ourselves. However, all too often, as children we're pushed in other directions and burdened with expectations that don't belong to us.

Eudora's experience with her daughter, Hanne, illustrates this. Hanne has always loved drawing and often loses track of time while she's doing it. She forgets to eat or drink and becomes lost in her own world. In fact, when things become overwhelming for her, drawing helps her reconnect to herself. It was when Hanne stopped drawing that Eudora realised there was a serious problem. 'Hanne was heading towards a breakdown,' Eudora remembers. 'She didn't want to go to school, and when she was there, she hid under the table. We knew we needed to do something but didn't know what. Then I discovered Hanne writing a list of the children in her class. She told me she was struggling with the pressure at school and that she wasn't the only one. She thought that if she got all the children in her class to sign this paper and brought it to the headteacher, they would do something about the pressure.' That's when Eudora, myself and Hanne's father decided to home-school her. When we found the perfect school for Hanne in Germany she started drawing again and expressing her creativity. She has now rediscovered her passion, flow and purpose.

> YOUR TURN: *In your journal, note the challenges you have faced as an individual and ask how these challenges have connected or reconnected you to your passion, your purpose, your flow, and your relationship to something greater than yourself.*

Connecting to your creative flow can produce extraordinary results, says Eudora: 'My creativity flows through me either into the thing I'm creating – whether it's a knitted jumper, a sewn scarf, a piece of writing or the work I'm doing with a client. When I'm in this flow, I feel amazing. Worries and insecurities melt away. It's as if I step out of the way and let something far greater than me express itself.' However, there are times when she's not in flow: 'In fact, I'm rather grumpy,' she says. 'In these moments, everything is hard. I break a cup, I forget to buy the very item I went into town to get, I almost bump the car, everything takes twice as long.'

> YOUR TURN: *Take a moment to think of times in your life when everything flowed, everything felt easy. And then think about moments when it didn't flow, when life seemed difficult. How did it feel in your body? What was different?*

If only we could capture the essence of what gets us into our flow and bottle it so that whenever we feel disconnected and grumpy, we could uncork the bottle and take a gulp of flow. Here's an exercise to help you start connecting to your flow.

> YOUR TURN: *Find a quiet space and time when you won't be disturbed. Put all your devices away and have your journal to hand. Sit comfortably, with an open body posture and your feet on the floor. Close your eyes and become aware of your breath. Take a deep breath in and a deep breath out. Become aware of your breath and your body. Taking another deep breath in, think back to when you were young. What were the things that you loved doing? When could you lose yourself and lose all sense of time? Travel back to the moments when you felt most connected to yourself and your environment. When you have connected to these memories, start writing. Don't think about what you're writing; let the pen do the work. Once you feel complete, put down your pen and read what you've written. Notice what jumps out of the page. What insights have you had?*

Business leaders and their purpose

To give you some further guidance on purpose, I asked each of the business leaders I interviewed about their purpose in life. I received a variety of answers, which goes to show how personal it is. Here are a few:

Rita Clifton, deputy chair John Lewis Partnership, chairman BrandCap and NED for a number of other companies: 'My fundamental personal purpose is that I'd like to save the world. I want to make the world a better place. It has been the same since I was seven, and I'm sure it'll be the same when I'm 70. To be more specific, I want to make business more human on every level – caring about the planet, about people, about helping society move forward. A big part of making businesses more human is making sure we have more women running organisations – to change the chemical balance at the top of all companies and nations. When you have 96 per cent of major organisations and 93 per cent of countries run by men, something is seriously out of whack. We need balance.'

Chris Martin, former Musgrave CEO, NED at Wilko, ABP Food Group and other companies: 'At this point my personal purpose is to give something back, to use my experience and skills. My business purpose is to use those skills to help businesses confront the challenges and opportunities ahead. Overall, it's to have some fun and to live a full-on family life alongside my business life.'

Justin King, former Sainsbury's CEO and NED at Marks & Spencer and other companies: 'My purpose is entirely self-serving – I look in the mirror and test whether I've done the best with the talents I've been given – and that I don't just use them for myself but also for my family and the community that I'm part of. It's my definition of self-actualisation, rather than a purpose.'

Charles Wilson, former Booker CEO: 'My personal purpose is that I like doing the job well.' (Charles told me it was a family joke that whether he is sweeping the yard, or running a company or a charity, he always wants to do a great job.)

Vittoria Varalli, VP of Canadian grocer Sobey's: 'My personal ethos is that I spend my life enabling the potential of others – both at work, to enable my team to become the best version of themselves, and outside work, where I am the interim chair of the UN Association of Canada. I feel passionate about the sustainable development goal on gender equality and take part in grassroots activity around this.'

Aileen Richards, NED at Samworth Brothers, Pret a Manger and other companies; former global head of People & Organisation at Mars: 'My personal purpose in a business context is to be really passionate with messages about the importance of good leadership, behaviours and talent – if you have that, anything is possible. It's to demonstrate that the world can be better through running good companies with good leadership.'

Roger Whiteside, CEO of Greggs: 'I have no idea what my purpose in life is. Yes, it does bother me and leads me into bigger questions. I'm 62 and still don't know what I want to do when I leave school! I've never known what I was going to do – I've always done what seems the right thing to do at the time, following the line of least resistance. I've had a great and enjoyable career in retailing – but it could've been anywhere. Is it too late? If I haven't got it so far, will I now? Maybe, maybe not!'

I love Roger's honesty – and it shows that you can have a successful career without knowing what your purpose is. However, if you want to be a heart-centred leader, I recommend that you do take the time to reflect on it if you can.

Personal purpose versus business purpose

One question I'm often asked is whether purpose relates to your work or your whole life. A number of the leaders quoted above make a distinction between business and personal purpose. My belief is that this separation is artificial. When I'm on the ski hill or walking in the woods pondering life – is that work or not? As I sit here writing, I'm working, but I'm also having fun and feeling energised. I feel my purpose relates to my whole life and that feels right. I encourage you to trust the process of finding your purpose and see what emerges over time. And if you have a burning desire for clarity, find yourself a training course or programme that can help you along your way. You could, for example, join our next Stepping into Your Authentic Leadership programme. We'll be looking at organisational purpose in Chapter 5.

Purpose beyond business

While this book is focused on business, I believe everything we say here can be applied to the whole of life. Looking at the world of sport, I'm reminded of a powerful interview with Formula 1 World Champion Lewis Hamilton on BBC Radio 4's *Today* programme in July 2021. He shared how he'd started to question his purpose: 'My whole life I've been driven to winning these races, and now I've been winning races and championships… it's very short lived when you win. You're then on to the next one. I've always wondered what it all means, why was I chosen to have the ability I have, to be the only black driver to get into this sport, and not only that, to be at the front. What does that really mean; what am I supposed to be doing with that?' He has started to address this issue with the Hamilton Commission, which he set up in 2019 to increase the representation of black people in F1. Of the 40,000 who currently work in the industry, only one per cent are black. He also recalled his time at school, when none of his teachers were black and he had no role models he could relate to: 'I look back at my young self and wish it had been different – if I could change that, that would be the most valuable thing for me personally.' He realised that creating this change was his life purpose, the reason why he was here. He ended the interview with: 'That would be my legacy.' While people don't usually think about their legacy until they're in their 50s, Hamilton stands out as impressive and forward-thinking at just 36. I believe that reflecting on your legacy is a way to focus on your purpose. What do you want to be remembered for? I'll answer this question from my own perspective in the final chapter.

A word about money

To conclude our investigation into personal purpose, I need to mention the m-word. I don't believe money can make you happy or that making money can be your purpose in life. In fact, every study I've seen shows that once you get beyond the basic amount you need to pay for a roof over your head, clothes on your back and food in your belly (the base of Maslow's hierarchy of needs), money doesn't make that much difference to your levels of happiness. If you look at studies about what people appreciate about their jobs, money rarely makes it into the top three. Factors such as being appreciated by your manager or colleagues, doing a job that makes a difference and working with people you like all tend to beat money every time.

In 2016, the UK Government replaced the minimum wage with the living wage and set a four-year timeline to move the hourly rate from £6.70 in stages to £9.00. This was absolutely the right thing to do – you try living on £6.70 per hour. As a store owner, it posed a challenge, as we were already paying above the minimum wage. Then Lidl made a bold move – they immediately raised everyone to the £9.00 level (versus stage one, which was £7.20), four years ahead of schedule. I know other independent retailers in London who lost plenty of people as a result, but we didn't lose a single person. Despite the attraction of £1.80 extra per hour (which at 25 per cent more is not inconsiderable), each of my team felt that the benefits of staying at Thornton's Budgens outweighed the extra cash. I have to say I was really proud of what we'd achieved in that moment.

Eudora has a different perspective on money, having experienced a period in her life when she was a single parent on benefits, with no secure housing and without the ability to earn money because she was caring for an 18-month-old child: 'I know what it's like to feel terrified about where the next £5 would come from,' says Eudora. 'Now I see that, like so many things, money will continue to remain unequal in a society that doesn't include or properly count women and ethnic minorities. In his book, *The Uncounted*, Alex Cobham wrote about these damaging inequalities; and in her book *Invisible Women*, Caroline Criado Perez wrote about the gender data gap that exists in society. This absence of data means that officially, legally and politically the uncounted don't exist. Ethnic minorities and women most often fall into the poorest bracket of society, so they are the most disenfranchised. However, evidence shows that when the invisible and uncounted are represented it saves society, governments and business money. Poor quality and missing data are impacting us all in far greater ways than we can imagine. We as a society have a choice to change this bias and save money at the same time.'

I do feel privileged that I've never had to worry about where the next £5 would come from. However, I know that several people who worked in the store sometimes experienced financial challenges. I remember one of the team sharing with me that he only had £3 in his bank account and two kids to feed, which makes it even more extraordinary that no one at Thornton's Budgens was tempted by the Lidl offer. We also had a couple of loan schemes in place, which helped people with everything from affording their next meal to getting on the property ladder. And while we always aimed to pay above the minimum wage, if I had my time again, I would have focused more on what we could have done to improve everyone's pay. I would have offered everyone a 10 per cent rise for three months, funded from reserves or by myself, on the basis that we'd then have had three months to work together to generate the additional sales/profit to cover the rise. If we hadn't succeeded, everyone's pay would have had to revert to the old levels. Although I believe that, with everyone's focus behind this goal of better pay, we would have generated those funds.

In Eudora's first interview with a member of the Thornton's Budgens team, Sadia talks about how job opportunities at the store provided her family with financial independence.

A quick comment about the team interviews. Eudora did these to ensure they were a bit more objective. When I first read them, I was very humbled, moved to tears and a bit embarrassed about publishing some of the gushing comments about me. I will live with that embarrassment, as they are speaking from the heart and sharing the impact of this journey on their lives.

Thornton's Budgens team interview #1

Name: Sadia Ahmed
Nationality: UK born Bangladeshi
Position: Cashier
Length of service: Four years (from the age of 16)

I was appointed an internal coach at Thornton's Budgens and received coaching myself during this time, which I found very helpful. It boosted my self-confidence and added value to what I was doing. There was a deep connection with my coach, who asked open-ended questions. I felt comfortable talking about any type of situation and it changed how I see the world. I started to think outside the box and was motivated to work harder. I wanted to meet the needs of the customer and started to think about how I could help other people. I felt I was part of a wider cause.

I knew I could always talk to my coach about any situation and that she'd help me see it from a different perspective. I started to look at things differently and realised I could solve things without being condescending or abrupt. I realised that difficult situations could be resolved calmly and collectively. I noticed my colleagues changing, too. They became aware of the bigger picture. They gained more respect for Andrew as they saw him helping people grow and supporting the community. They saw that even when Andrew was struggling and facing financial strain, he was there for the team and the community. They saw that Andrew was making a difference.

The staff faced stressful situations when customers were unhappy that the self-checkouts didn't work properly, or the plastic-free bags broke. We set about seeing the positive and creating solutions. These kinds of challenging situations brought us together. We learnt to communicate better. This approach to coaching and growth has given me hope. I know there are good people out there who aren't just interested in profit but who also consider the health and professional development of their people. Andrew's approach to business has motivated me to help others.

I feel a deep gratitude towards Andrew. He gave my mother a job and believed in her when she was at her lowest. She was unqualified and a single mother. His continued support of my mother meant that there was always food on our table. Other members of my family also worked in Thornton's Budgens. This was our first experience of work and was our starting point towards financial independence. People often don't consider why someone wants a job. When Andrew gave my mother a job, he gave the whole family hope.

 **3**

The Foundations of Authentic Leadership

The concept of Authentic Leadership that Eudora and I have developed has evolved over six years of trial and error. It builds on my 10-plus years of personal development work and many more years than that for Eudora. I'm aware that Authentic Leadership is a term that's being used more and more in business – so when I use those words, with initial capitals, I'm referring to the specific approach we have developed. We haven't protected the intellectual property for this approach as we both believe in open-source sharing. Eudora defines Authentic Leadership as: 'Leaders who are genuine, self-aware, transparent and live out all parts of their lives with integrity.' She believes that we can all choose to be leaders in our lives.

This chapter outlines the background to Authentic Leadership and gives you a series of exercises that you can complete to help you become more authentic in the way that you lead. Our work is a blend of many different models and concepts, so what follows is our take on how we function as human beings, inspired by what we've personally observed at work. It has helped us better understand our inner workings and therefore how to help people develop their leadership.

1. Identifying triggers

Once you have reflected on your purpose and how you might achieve a state of flow, it's vital to develop your psychological and emotional self-awareness. This is about how you deal with and process your emotions, how you respond to others and how you behave. In fact, awareness is the first step towards changing how you react and respond to life. With awareness comes choice – the choice to change how you approach your life. Without awareness, you can't make that choice.

We'll start with triggers. Triggers are emotional reactions, often strong bodily reactions to external or internal stimuli. We perceive those stimuli as either positive or negative. There are three types of trigger: external (taking place outside your body), internal (taking place inside your mind) and deliberately self-created. Though the experience is either external or in your mind, the reaction is an emotional response felt in the body. Eudora has found that initially many of her clients are unaware of their bodily reactions but, over time, they rediscover how to listen to their body and emotions. Then they start to have a choice about how to respond to a situation or stimulus. The first two types of trigger can't be controlled, but can be understood and mastered. The advantage of the last type is that you can self-create a trigger from a predetermined stimulus or situation. Understanding why you're reacting to a situation gives you self-awareness and choice. You can decide to make a change by using the information that the trigger is giving you, responding differently and making more productive decisions.

One of our greatest sources of learning has been COR, the US-based personal growth company. We have both attended many of their training programmes and I now have the honour of being part of their leadership team as a non-executive director (NED). Founders Britta and Lee Eskey look at triggers this way: 'Staying mindful when we're triggered is a hard thing to do. We may need something stronger than simply tracking our body sensations – we may even need to create some.'

They suggest doing the following exercise when you feel triggered: *Press your feet into the ground, rub your hands together, do some stretching or exercise. Take deeper breaths into the belly. You may even splash some cold water on your face, get some air or safely let out some intense emotion.*

You can begin to understand why you get triggered by looking at how your brain functions. There's still a lot that we don't know about the brain, but we do know that it is divided into three parts: the neocortex, the limbic system and the primitive brain. The neocortex is the thinking part of our brain, where creativity and the ability to lie coexist. This is the part of the brain that makes us human. The limbic system is the unconscious, reactive part of the brain where triggers occur. It responds to the world around you and stores memories. By going deeper into how the limbic system works, you can find ways to understand and control your triggers. This part of the brain has evolved in order to respond to and stay alive in dangerous situations. This is often referred to as the fight, flight or freeze response – but there's also a mechanism to enhance positive experiences. Eudora explains: 'Imagine a child reading a book. As they do this, they might be twirling their hair, sucking their thumb or stroking their ear. These actions are enriching the experience and creating a pacifier, also known as an adaptive behaviour. The child is unconsciously creating a link between a positive experience and a pacifier. It's in moments of stress that the pacifier or adaptive behaviour reappears as a form of coping mechanism to help the child feel less stressed.'

The limbic system automatically creates a link between a positive experience and a pacifier/adaptive behaviour. You can use this process to consciously create a connection so that when you experience an event or situation, it automatically links to a particular reaction. You're actually creating a trigger. This is useful because you can change how you react to a stimulus. If you do this enough times, you can create a new habit and change an old pattern.

2. The HEAL process

The process Eudora uses to create links in her brain is based on what happens naturally in the limbic system. Developed by Rick Hanson, it's called the HEAL process (the acronym is from the first letter of each step), and it can help you create a positive experience and avoid negative triggers.

YOUR TURN: *Find a quiet place where you won't be disturbed. Sit comfortably, with an open body posture, and close your eyes. Take a deep breath in and a deep breath out. Become aware of your breath. Bring your breath deep into the base of your belly.*

Step 1: Have or think of a positive experience – *one that you're experiencing right now, a memory, something you've read in a book or seen in a film, or even something you've made up. It doesn't matter, as they all sit in the same place in your brain. What's important is that you can fully experience it with all your senses.*

Step 2: Enrich it – *stay in this experience and then spend 5-10 seconds longer in it. Open up your body and all your senses to the experience. Notice what you can see, taste, touch, smell and hear.*

Step 3: Absorb it – *allow yourself to be completely submerged in the experience and become the experience. At this point you can choose to stop and enjoy the experience* *or go to step 4, where you actively create a link with a difficult or negative experience and create a new reaction.*

***Step 4: Link positive and negative material** – choose a difficult situation where you'd like to experience a different reaction. While remaining deeply in the positive experience, take a deep breath and open your body and senses to this positive experience. Take another deep breath in and a deep breath out. Focus only a small amount of attention on the difficult or negative experience that's in the background. Consciously make a link between the positive and the negative experience knowing that all is well.*

Eudora created a new relationship with her panic attacks by using the above process. 'I hate crossing bridges, flying, walking through long tunnels or standing near very tall buildings,' she explains. 'Sometimes, when I am travelling on my own, I become completely overwhelmed and my system starts to shut down. As a child I learnt that it was dangerous to express too much emotion in front of other people, so when I'm in the middle of a panic attack, the last thing I want to do is ask a stranger for help. Once I've had a panic attack in a particular place or situation, it becomes harder to return there, as I'm frightened that it will happen again.'

She knew she needed to make a change and decided to use every opportunity to link positive emotions to the negative situations and places: 'One evening Andrew and I attended a black tie awards ceremony,' she recalls. 'As we were leaving the Tube station, I had a flashback to a memory of me having a panic attack at this very same station. I asked Andrew if we could stop for a moment. I held his arm and felt the strength and warmth of his body next to mine. I breathed in the night air and opened my body to experience the moment with all my senses. And then I looked up at the tall buildings, creating a link between the buildings and the positive experience I was having.' As a result, she enjoyed the awards evening, and every time she noticed herself enjoying it, she repeated the 'have, enrich and absorb' steps of the process. Try it yourself and see how you get on.

At the end of this chapter, you can read the second of Eudora's interviews with key members of the team at Thornton's Budgens. Kate has worked on her triggers and says that she now takes time to evaluate a situation at work before responding.

3. Our shadows

If you watch young kids at play, they're full of the joys of spring – in the moment and totally free. They fall, they cry, they pick themselves up and start playing again. Then, at around the age of seven, we start to become aware of norms and how other people would like us to behave. Parents and teachers say things like 'Big boys don't cry' or 'Don't get angry' and 'Don't be sad, everything will be fine.' We start to pick up the message that it's not OK to cry, be angry or sad. These become emotions and behaviours we want to avoid, and they disappear into what Carl Jung first described as the shadow. The desire to cry, be angry or sad doesn't go away; it just goes out of our conscious awareness.

As kids, we're often told not to be selfish – but there are aspects of selfishness that are important, such as self-care (see Chapter 4). When my kids were young, there was always a lot to be done at home – yet three or four times a week, I would make sure I went running to keep myself fit. Every time I did that, I could've been accused of being selfish, yet I believed that I needed to keep myself in shape to be the best father, boss, colleague and husband I could be. Selfish or self-care?

I grew up in Ireland, where the general attitude was: 'Don't be angry, be happy – and shit happens.' I spent years suppressing my anger, as I felt it wouldn't be welcome. Instead of it going away, it leaked out in a passive-aggressive way – which is deeply unpleasant for anyone on the receiving end. What I've learnt, only recently, is that it's better to express my anger cleanly and clearly – 'I'm really angry because you said we were going to have a date night tonight and at the last minute you said some work had come up and you needed to cancel' – rather than sulk. My learning has been dramatically improved by living with Eudora and Hanne because Germans don't understand why you would not just say it how it is. It's hard to take sometimes, but refreshing when you get used to it. So, anger often hides in my shadow, along with the 'good boy'. When I was growing up, like many, our household was a busy one. I was the eldest of four; my father was involved in exporting and travelled a lot. So, to get my parents' attention, I developed the 'good boy' strategy – thinking that if I was really good, helpful and unselfish, I'd get more attention. It's a reasonable and fairly common strategy to have as a child. However, without realising it, I took the good boy into my adult life and tried to please everyone, even if they didn't ask me to, and then I'd (passive-aggressively) resent them for it.

As we move into adulthood, it's important that we understand which childhood strategies we developed to gain love and evaluate whether they're still appropriate. Jung has developed a whole body of work around the shadow, where the principle is that if you can see your shadow, it won't trip you up – but if you can't, it will! My tendency to be a good boy will never go away – but now I have the awareness to spot it, generally before I over-commit. Sometimes I just smile to myself, and at other times I will share with someone that I've noticed there is a (younger) part of me that wants to please them by doing XYZ.

> YOUR TURN: *See if you can identify a recurring behaviour of yours, something you do so often that if you were really honest about it, you'd rather you didn't do it. Notice it and observe it in action – even share it with one or two people close to you. See how it feels to do this.*

If you'd like to dig deeper into this subject, an excellent starting point is *Warrior, Magician, Lover, King* by Rod Boothroyd (see Resources).

4. The inner critic

Ever hear that voice inside your head telling you that you are useless, rubbish and don't deserve to be in this job/relationship? This is the inner critic – the voice that gnaws away at our self-confidence. In his excellent book on the subject, *Make Peace with Your Mind*, Mark Coleman describes some of his early discoveries about the inner critic: 'It was the practice of mindfulness that made me aware of the tyrannical self-judgments that were making my life miserable.' He went on to recognise how hard he was on himself and the impossibly high standards he had set for himself. Sound familiar? As with your shadow, it's good to get to know your inner critic and befriend them. Mine is called Dirk. And while we know each other well and mostly work things out together, there are times when he takes over and gives me hell. And he can also affect how I am with others. When he's in the driving seat, we're never going to get anywhere. When I was discussing this with Rita Clifton from the John Lewis Partnership, she told me: 'I have this constant fear of running out of money. Even though I'm past 60, and busier than I've ever been, the imposter on my shoulder says: "You can't do that – you'll get found out." And even though we have more money than my parents could ever have dreamed of, I'm always worrying we're going to lose it – because I lost a parent at 12 and we were left in a lot of debt. I always worried money would disappear, so there's a drive to keep on earning.'

What is your inner critic/imposter telling you? If this subject touches you and you'd like some more help with getting to know your inner critic, I can highly recommend Mark Coleman's book.

> YOUR TURN: *Tune in and listen to some of your internal voices and write down what they have to say. Is any of it true? Really? Can you really have come this far in life by being so useless?*

5. Ego states

An Authentic Leader needs to develop an awareness of their ego states. In this context, ego is defined as: 'A person's self-image, self-esteem and self-importance.' Ego states emerged through a theory developed by Eric Berne, the founder of transactional analysis (TA). He divided the ego into three parts: the Child, the Adult and the Parent. He said we are always acting from at least one of these parts and that this leads to a reaction in the person we're interacting with.

- 💜 The **Child** ego state kicks in when we feel bad, childlike or anxious. It's connected to our memories and the ways in which we behaved when we were young. When we're in our Child, we respond immaturely to situations. How we felt, thought and behaved as a child gets replayed, even when we're adults.

- 💜 In the **Adult** ego state, we're rational, aware of our surroundings and our body. Our feelings and actions are appropriate to the situation that we find ourselves in. When we're in our Adult, we can pause and think through how to respond in a rational way. We're aware of ourselves and our impact on others.

- 💜 In the **Parent** ego state, we find ourselves feeling, talking and thinking like one of our parents or significant parental figures. We can go into Parent if the emotion that's triggered is one that a parent also had. If your father was an angry man, then you might behave like him when you're angry. We react rather than think in a situation. These behaviours are copied, learnt or borrowed from significant parental figures.

Your ego state has an effect on those around you. If you're in your Adult, then this encourages others to respond from their Adult. If you're in your Child, this can trigger those with whom you interact and can invite them unconsciously to respond by going into their Parent. If you're in your Parent, this can awaken Child behaviour in those with whom you interact. 'I've noticed that if I go out into the world and interact from my Adult, then my day flows and I have healthy, productive exchanges with others,' explains Eudora, who is qualified in the use of TA. 'However, if I'm triggered and find myself in either Parent or Child, then those around me respond to that state by taking the opposite position. In my Child, perhaps feeling rebellious, I might be met with a controlling Parent. Or if I become a righteous Parent, I might be met by an immature Child.'

I remember a time when I was feeling overwhelmed by my never-ending to-do list. On top of that our week had been turned upside-down with Hanne being unwell and off school, and it was the day of my weekly visit to the local food market in Germany, which was the last thing I needed to do. I'll let Eudora tell the story: 'Andrew's overwhelm was stopping him from being present, grounded and in his Adult. I knew from experience that going to a busy market and having to speak German was going to end badly if he approached it from this triggered state. So, he talked through what he was feeling overwhelmed about, meditated, went for a swim in our local lake and promised himself a hot chocolate at the end of his foraging. He let go of his overwhelm and the things he couldn't control, connected to nature, exercised and did something he loved. He ended up having several connected experiences at the market and even spoke a lot of German. A man even jumped out of his car while they were queuing at a traffic light to tell Andrew how smart he was to have a tow bar on his cabriolet!' It's from this Adult place that you can develop self-awareness, which then gives you choices.

> YOUR TURN: *Take a moment to consider how you can resource yourself and what you can do to put yourself into your Adult ego state. Think of a recent example of when you were grounded, in flow, in your healthy Adult. What did it feel like? How could you work on doing this more often?*

We humans are not consistent. We tend to move from one state to the next without even realising it. However, with awareness and self-knowledge we can understand why we're experiencing a trigger, then pause and choose how we respond to it. Transactional analysis expert Rosemary Napper, author of *Tactics* and director of TAWorks, told Eudora: 'It's only from our Adult that we're able to lead. We need to inhabit our Adult to learn, stay present, become self-aware and discover who we are as a leader. It's here that our passion can be awakened, and we find our individual style of leading. To lead, you need to know your unique purpose, which can only be discovered from the Adult ego state.'

6. Inflated and deflated ego

Now we can dive deeper into the ego and divide it into two types: the inflated ego and the deflated ego. Instead of seeing ourselves exactly as we are, we can either inflate how we see ourselves, for example thinking we're the cleverest person in the room; or we can see ourselves as deflated, a lesser version of who we really are. Perhaps we have an inner critic that says: 'You're a waste of space. No one would notice if you weren't here.' We can find ourselves imagining that we have no purpose, that we are invisible. We all have an inflated and a deflated ego, but one tends to be more dominant than the other. Eudora tells the story of her inflated ego, which she sees as Wonder Woman, ready to save the world at any moment.

'One of the most memorable days of my working life was 7 July 2005, the day of the London bombings. I was locking up my bike when I heard a loud pop. It was only when I heard the news and saw a lot of people standing near my office building looking lost that I started to realise what was going on. All the roads were blocked and there was no mobile phone signal. I didn't realise at the time how close I had come to being caught up in the bus explosion as I cycled to work. It was clear to me that I needed to persuade senior staff to stop working and open the building to the thousands of people who had become stranded. We opened the doors, offered free tea and coffee to everyone as well as free use of our landlines so that people could contact their loved ones and tell them they were safe. That day I really did feel like a superhero. My inflated ego was able to jump into action and make a real difference to many people's lives.'

In the right context, such as this one, the inflated ego can be powerful and useful. However, it can also come out when it's not needed and make situations worse. For example, you could help an old woman across the street without asking her if she actually wanted to cross the street. The same goes for our deflated ego. It can help us stay grounded and reflective, but also lead us into believing that we're not OK.

7. I'm OK, you're OK

Eudora grew up in an environment that she found frightening and at times terrifying. 'I never knew, from one minute to the next, how my mother would react to me. Would she respond with anger or with love? I developed patterns of behaviour that helped me cope in this unpredictable situation.' As a result, she learnt how to read other people and situations. For example, she was able to read her mother's mood by her body language and tone of voice. Growing up, she tried everything to gain her love, to make her OK. Eric Berne talks about everyone being born good, or OK, and that our individual life experiences teach us to see the world as a series of interactions between OK and not OK. Psychiatrist Frank Ernst developed this premise into the OK Corral, which looks at interactions between you and another person. In all interactions with another person, one of four dynamics take place:

1. **I'm OK, you're not OK:** In this position the person feels superior to others. They may be contemptuous and quick to anger. Parents and managers can find themselves in this position. They try to be perfect and tend to respond with 'fight' behaviours.

2. **I'm not OK, you're OK:** In this position the person feels inferior to others. They tend to have low self-esteem and put others first. They try to please others and tend to respond with 'flight' behaviours.

3. **I'm not OK, you're not OK:** This position is rare. The person feels bad and also projects badness on the other. There's a sense of betrayal and retribution in this dynamic. They tend to respond with 'freeze' behaviours.

4. **I'm OK, you're OK:** This is the ideal position with a sense of comfort and ease apparent in any interactions. These are happy, confident people who get on with others even if there's a difference of opinion. They tend to respond with authentic behaviours and come across as being in flow.

Parenting and family systems educator Jean Illsley Clarke developed this model further. When we're leading from the 'I'm OK, you're OK' quadrant, we can experience flow, a win–win dynamic and can be authentically ourselves. In the other quadrants we experience the anxiety responses of flight, freeze and fight and enter a lose–win, lose–lose or win–lose dynamic. As Rosemary Napper told Eudora: 'Our experiences of bad leaders prove more helpful. It's through the difficult experiences that we discover the good leader in us. An Authentic Leader invites us to join them in the Adult ego state. An Authentic Leader is always learning, growing and maximising the potential in their team.' She also asks the question:

what does OK-ness mean to you? For Rosemary, it's this: 'Respect and value. So, I respect and value myself, and I respect and value you as a human being, even though I might not appreciate your behaviour or agree with your ideas.'

> YOUR TURN: *In your journal, write down what OK-ness means to you – both in how you relate to yourself and how you relate to others.*

8. Growing into 'I'm OK, you're OK'

Eudora's early childhood experience was one of 'I'm not OK, you're not OK'. She remembers: 'I tried everything to make my mother OK so that she would love me and care for me. When my mother was angry at me, I would freeze. I remember thinking that if I crossed all my fingers behind my back, then everything would be OK. It wasn't. I spent a lot of my early childhood feeling frozen and scared.' She went to a Quaker boarding school from the age of 10 and developed a number of positive parental relationships with teachers and boarding house staff, and was surprised that they took the trouble to listen to her and take her seriously. 'My relationship with my mother worsened as I became a teenager. I moved into a dynamic of 'I'm not OK, you're OK' and realised that if I didn't want to disappear and have my soul die, I needed to leave. I went into flight mode.' As a result, she has an overdeveloped ability to read others, to ensure that they are OK, but: 'I'm not very good at looking at my own needs and making myself OK. It has taken me many years and a lot of self-development to move from the dynamic of 'I'm not OK, you're OK' where I'm in constant flight mode to one of 'I'm OK, you're OK', where life is in flow.'

A word about self-leadership

A heartful business needs to have an 'I'm OK, you're OK' culture; in other words an authentic, win–win attitude, if it is to thrive and develop. Self-leadership was the way we chose to develop this culture at Thornton's Budgens. While the story of how this unfolded is told in Chapter 7, for now I'll define self-leadership as 'becoming an expert on yourself through a commitment to honest self-reflection and the ongoing process of learning and growing from your experiences'. It's a powerful way to start your journey towards becoming an Authentic Leader.

Coaching played a huge role in our self-leadership work at Thornton's Budgens. It's a tool that can help people grow and develop. In the early days, we trained four internal coaches. One of them ran an in-flow exercise with Seelan, our produce (fruit and veg) manager. He said that he was very good at and loved being creative, especially with in-store displays. When asked by his coach why he hadn't acted on this yet, Seelan recalled having built a display earlier in his career and being told by the store manager that it was rubbish. He immediately put the idea of bringing his creativity to work into the category of 'something it's not safe to do', and it became a core wound. Encouraged by his coach, Seelan started to build some small tomato displays at the entrance to the store. Having had great feedback from me and others, he built larger displays until the tomato displays at Thornton's Budgens became famous! Local people even took photos of their new-born babies next to our tomatoes and posted them on Facebook. As a result, our tomato sales increased, as did our total produce sales. Seelan also grew in confidence and became much more engaged with customers and his colleagues. Inspired by his approach, others started to build their own displays. That's quite an amazing set of outcomes from one coaching session!

Here are a couple of the lessons we learnt about coaching:

1. Use of external coaches can be pivotal, both at the kick-off stage and when you want to make a big shift in behaviour. For example, we used a group of Human Potential coaches (see Chapter 7) to work with the team

as part of the transition from command and control to self-leadership.

2. In the long term, it's important to train up internal coaches. At Thornton's Budgens, that evolved into a coaching style of leadership, with ad hoc (external) coaching available for people who needed additional support. We found having internal coaches led to increased ownership of the work culture and an increase in psychological safety.

However, coaching must be voluntary. You can't force people to open their hearts; it has to come naturally. Despite knowing this, at one point I tried to impose coaching on the whole self-leadership team. Needless to say, I received pushback from those who didn't want to be coached at that time. Eudora has found that for those who are more resistant to being coached, using their Human Potential Assessment (see Chapter 7) as a starting point and inviting them to choose a dimension to look at provides a gentler approach than coaching. She also found that an internal coach can be better received and seen more as a motivational cheerleader for people who are resistant to coaching.

Eudora noticed a change at Thornton's Budgens as a result of the coaching: 'As more and more team members were coached and discovered that they were welcome to bring all of themselves to work, the internal culture changed. The traditional cultural divisions along national and faith lines started to fade and a merging took place. Individuals felt empowered to trust themselves to make decisions without asking permission, and a culture of communicating ideas and appreciation started to flourish. The staff became a team, individuals felt safe to be themselves at work and creativity flowed.'

As you'll see in the interview that follows, Kate experienced positive changes at home as well as at work as a result of the coaching she received, which in turn made her a more effective team member.

Thornton's Budgens team interview #2

Name: Kate Avgarska
Nationality: Bulgarian
Position: Co-leader
Length of service: Nine years, plus 12 with another Budgens store and at head office

The changes that have occurred because of the coaching at Thornton's Budgens were not initially obvious to the outside world. They were gradual and took at least 12 months to become noticeable. I've certainly become more aware of my own emotions as well as those of my co-workers. I've become a better team leader and listener. Before the coaching, I didn't show my daughters what was going on for me. Now I allow them to see my emotions. The coaching has brought me closer to my daughters; we have more appreciation for each other now.

I've also learnt to remain calm, to step back from a situation and evaluate it before I respond. Last year I experienced a few challenging situations at work and noticed that I was able to respond differently. I was able to trust my instincts and stand by my decisions. I'm much more approachable now and aware of my impact on others. Now, when I'm faced with a co-worker who has a different opinion to me, we are able to voice our differences and explore solutions together instead of arguing.

The biggest challenge for me has been showing my vulnerability. My old behaviour pattern was to ignore my surroundings and just react. Today things are different;

there is now a culture of fairness. We are the Thornton's Budgens team, and we trust each other. We've known each other for a long time now and this increase in trust has brought us closer together. It moves situations on so that we can get more done.

Thornton's Budgens has moved to a new level of self-leadership. We're all moving towards the same goal, together. We give each other space to express our emotions, without making judgements. There's no fear of the consequences and we can openly offer each other emotional support. I feel more balanced and in harmony with myself. I can clearly see the achievements of the past two years. I've gone through some very big personal and professional changes. Covid has been a challenge, but it has made us stronger, together.

Becoming an Authentic Leader

By this point I hope you'll have an idea of what it takes to become an Authentic Leader. We've already shared plenty of exercises to help you shift into a more authentic version of yourself. The rest of the book is full of tools you can use on your own or with teams of people, be that at work, at home or at your local sports club. Being an Authentic Leader is hard and takes effort and courage. It also takes plenty of practice. It's a life's work – and I mean that in a positive sense, in that there are always new things to learn and areas to develop. An Authentic Leader models the ways of being that your organisation needs to have in place in order to deliver on its purpose. And with the right leadership, everyone in the organisation can be authentically themselves, leading to an 'I'm OK, you're OK' culture.

Eudora and I have developed the 10 principles of an Authentic Leader. If I had to sum them up in three words, it would be 'to be yourself'. It's also about being present in the now, rather than caught up in the past. This is the foundation of Authentic Leadership and means stripping back all of those defences you have built up during your life so far.

The 10 principles of an Authentic Leader

1. **Be your purpose:** To be a truly Authentic Leader, you need to be clear on your purpose – why you're here, why you get up in the morning and what the whole point of your life is. And then live from that place.

2. **Be in flow:** This is defined as doing what you love and are really good at. Within Thornton's Budgens, we focused on making sure most people in the organisation spent as much time as possible in flow. Happy people who are in flow will energise your business.

3. **Be of integrity:** I believe that you need to be in a state of integrity with yourself and others. That means being congruent with your values and beliefs, and it starts with being honest with yourself. In my case, it means being honest that I have a tendency to want to please people. Being in integrity with others is crucial to so many aspects of business life and would have prevented some of the chronic business failings of recent times.

4. **Be clear and consistent**: about who you are and what you stand for. If you do this, people will know where they stand with you and be willing to follow you. I know that my personal clarity helped me to bring the Thornton's Budgens team with me on an amazing journey. Over the past 14 years, the clearer and more consistent I've become, the easier it has been to bring others with me. You also need to be clear in your communication – both in what you say and in what you leave unsaid. Be firm about what's important to you. Having difficult

conversations is one of the most challenging things in life. I know (from painful experience) that avoiding difficult conversations leads to resentment, which leaks out in passive-aggressive ways – and for me that's the opposite of clear and clean communication. It's hard to have those conversations but worth finding ways in which to do so (see Tool 1 in the section that follows).

5. **Be organised:** In today's 24/7 e-world, it's easy to become overwhelmed and let some balls drop. Being in flow, clear on your purpose and able to have difficult conversations will help you set boundaries that will in turn help you to be more organised. If you're unreliable and chaotic, it's almost impossible to be an effective Authentic Leader.

6. **Be appreciative:** Appreciating people is one of the easiest ways to build relationships and help people feel valued. An Authentic Leader appreciates people every day and does it naturally, not just for gain. They do it on the basis that it's the right thing to do (see Tool 2).

7. **Be humble:** Humility is one of the most underrated leadership qualities. Too many leaders are too full of themselves – and that doesn't encourage people to open up to you. Barack Obama is a great role model for humility. A BBC film crew followed him around during his last year in office, and as well as discussing his successes, he often talked about how things didn't go to plan and how he might've done things differently – not something one could imagine his successor in the White House ever doing.

8. **Be vulnerable:** Having the ability to say 'I don't know' or 'I'm scared or really in pain' allows you to be honest and show your moral principles. For me, vulnerability creates trust and psychological safety. Combined with

humility, people will want to be with you, share with you and trust you when you show your vulnerability. It's the opposite of the stereotypical alpha male leader.

9. **Be present:** Being in the present moment means being fully with what's happening right now – the opposite of which is being caught up in the past. How often do you find yourself in your mind, thinking about stuff that happened years ago or worrying about the future? Or in a conversation, planning what you're going to say when the other person finishes speaking? Being fully present at all times is easy to say and really hard to do.

10. **Be trusting:** I added this principle after I sold the Belsize Park store. In discussions with the team during my leaving process, the most significant aspect of the heart journey for them was the trust that they felt from me and the leadership team – trust that helped them to grow their confidence and truly be themselves, knowing it was safe to do so.

With these principles in place, leaders can then create an organisational culture that enables people to be in flow. In his excellent book, *The Fourth Bottom Line*, Paul Hargreaves shares 50 leadership characteristics that he believes are needed today – to put it into my own words, to be an open-hearted Authentic Leader. I would strongly recommend his book as a way of building on the foundations we have laid out here.

One note of caution – it's easy to feel overwhelmed by all of this, as there's only so much change that our systems can cope with at any one time. Maybe everything in this book is new to you, or maybe you've come across some of the ideas and tools before. Whatever is true for you, be gentle with yourself. Work on the areas you feel drawn to and focus on those for now. And once you've mastered a few new ways of being, come back and choose something else to explore.

A word about vulnerability

As you may have guessed from the 10 principles, I believe that vulnerability is one of the most underrated leadership qualities and plays an important part in creating a heart-centred business. There's no better way to build trust with someone than to say things like 'I'm afraid, I don't know what we should do here' or 'I screwed up, I'm so sorry for what I said to you yesterday.' How many of you have felt anything like this over the past few months? And if you did, did you dare to share that with anyone? And how was it? If you didn't, can you imagine how it might have been?

> YOUR TURN: *Do it now. Choose someone and share something vulnerable – start small and with someone you trust and see how you get on.*

The best non-fiction book I have read recently was Rita Clifton's *Love Your Imposter*. She shows such vulnerability that, when I finished it, all I wanted to do was give her the biggest hug imaginable – and she's funny too. I learnt lots, laughed lots and would (even more than before) trust her with my life.

Our Authentic Leadership laboratory

Back in 2015, we decided that Thornton's Budgens would be the laboratory for our work, and we'd spend the next few years developing and testing ideas there. My poor team in Belsize Park – I'm not sure they knew what had hit them – but from the outset they were amazing and prepared to go deeply into this experiment. The fact that a majority of the team originated from the Indian subcontinent helped – as a heart-centred way of being is more common in the East than in the West. I only recently realised the impact of the sector I'd chosen to experiment in. Both Thornton's Budgens stores housed the most wonderful ethnic mix of people. When I owned both stores and we employed more than 150 people, there were no more than three or four purely British people working there. We had people from almost 50 different countries working in our stores.

As my long-standing colleague Shanthy (who is from Sri Lanka) shares below, I was the 'white man' leader whom it was too risky to challenge. Add to this the traditional command-and-control approach of the supermarket sector, and the fact that, despite our best endeavours to pay everyone reasonably well, the average wage in the sector was still low, I couldn't have chosen a more challenging place to invite people to open their hearts. There were times when the ideals I held as a privileged white man were so far away from the day-to-day reality of team members in the store. In fact, they were just not appropriate. A supermarket is a low-margin business. In London you'll pay huge rents – and every bit of space has to be used to sell. Many of my team had two jobs and were supporting their families in the UK as well as their extended family back home, and many were single mums. What I did offer them, though, was a chance to grow and develop as people – by trusting them, by giving them tools, and by creating a safe environment in which they could flourish.

Shanthy's story

Of all the interviews Eudora conducted with members of the team at Thornton's Budgens, Shanthy Lal's had the most profound impact on me. Shanthy has worked alongside me for almost 30 years. Ever since she joined SRCG as a part-time bookkeeper, she has managed the money side of my businesses. Her story shaped how we approached this book.

'I was 21 years old when I arrived in England,' Shanthy told Eudora. 'I was about to go to university and study business studies in my own country, Sri Lanka, but our family needed to leave immediately due to the political situation, so instead of becoming a student, I became a refugee. In the evenings I worked in a laundrette, washing sheets for hospitals and hotels; during the day I learnt English. I was lucky that I was taught English at a school that also taught us about English culture.

'When I got married my husband encouraged me to study accountancy on the weekends. I became pregnant, which delayed my studies. Then I was contacted by a job centre that told me about a part-time bookkeeping position in Richmond. I hadn't quite finished my accountancy studies but decided to apply for the position. I was terrified because I felt I lacked so many skills.

'I was given the bookkeeping position at SRCG in September 1992. Andrew was in charge of finance, and fortunately for me he was going on holiday shortly after I started my new job. This bought me time to get to grips with the role, and get to know the people in the team that I could rely on. I remember asking a lot of people for support during the first few months.

'When I first met Andrew, I saw him as just a boss. I felt I needed to be polite. I hoped he'd keep me on as a bookkeeper, but didn't have the courage to speak up. I felt I needed to look up to white people and that they were more powerful than us. I also felt they didn't take us seriously. I grew up in a culture where you respect the elders, always accepting, never questioning. How you treat your elders is viewed as a reflection of how well your parents brought you up. You'd never dream of questioning your boss on anything.

'When I fell pregnant with my third baby, I was frightened I might lose my job. Andrew still jokes that when I was about to give birth, I rang to let him know that I'd be sending him the cash flow report in advance of going to the hospital! That shows how worried I was. Andrew moved into sales but would still ask for financial information. Otherwise, I didn't have much to do with him for a few years.

'I remember he was always coming up with ideas and innovative ways of working. There would always be a new book that he'd want us to read. He was always introducing different ways of looking at communication and business. I remember the staff would joke and say: "Not another one, please! What happened to the last idea?" I went along with it because Andrew was the MD. It wasn't cool to admit we were benefiting from his ideas, but unconsciously we were growing.

'During this time, I passed all my accountancy exams, and the company grew. Through my hard work I was promoted to finance manager and then finance controller. A while later, Andrew decided to leave but I stayed at the consultancy. During the discussions about his exit plan, I became the go-between with Andrew and the other directors. I found myself disagreeing with Andrew, but finally an agreement was reached, and he bought the two Budgens stores.

'We kept in touch over the next eight months. Then, out of the blue, I found out Andrew was having an issue with his finances. Would I be willing to spend a day a week looking at his numbers? I'd never worked in retail before and felt nervous about being good enough. Andrew broke down the essence of retail: goods arrive at the back door; you sell them at the front door. What happens in between is the profit. Andrew wanted to understand why the store wasn't making a profit. Initially I had a six-month contract, but I discovered some big holes in the accounts and ended up staying on, managing the finances for both stores. When the consultancy firm closed down, I stayed on as a consultant for Andrew.

'When Andrew sold the Crouch End store, he put me in charge and gave me power of attorney to manage and finalise the sale of the store. I was surprised by his trust. It was a turning point. I thought back to the man I'd first met in 1992, about how intimidated I felt at the time. The dynamics had changed; the same man trusted me now. He left me in charge of managing his assets for three months. I stepped up and grew in confidence. I took on more responsibility and Andrew started to ask my opinion on staffing matters. Initially I didn't understand why he was asking for my opinion. This was new territory for me – but the more he trusted me, the more I did a better job for him.

'I found the sale of Crouch End stressful as I'd become close to the team. It was very emotional when I left. I remember ringing Andrew and telling him I was upset that he hadn't asked me how I felt about the sale of the store; he just wanted to know that the deal was done. He apologised. He said he should've cared about my feelings. I found I had the courage to call him out on his actions. I was able to hold him to account, and he was able to apologise. My relationship with the white man changed.

'I was involved in the overall management at the Belsize Park store. Andrew became more involved in the

Heart in Business work. He trusted me to be in control of finance. He felt if the financial side was in good shape, then everything else would be taken care of. I eventually became good with people. I discovered I could speak up if I felt the staff weren't being treated fairly. Andrew was able to concentrate on developing Heart in Business because I was keeping an eye on the day-to-day running of the store.

'I found the Stepping into Your Authentic Leadership training really useful. I started to look at things differently. I wanted to know why someone might be doing something and reacting in a certain way. People come to me with their issues now. I try to be balanced, fair and do the right thing.

'I sometimes clash with Andrew and disagree with his decisions. For example, I remember him trying to implement a sleep tracker programme in the store. He wanted to reward staff who'd had a good night's sleep because then they'd do a better job at work. I didn't think this was a good idea. Many of the staff have second jobs to support their families. I felt that rewarding people who slept well would encourage cheating from those who couldn't get enough sleep because of their second jobs. It would also reward the wrong people – people who had the luxury of time to sleep. Some of Andrew's ideas were disconnected from the reality of the lives of the people working in the store. I played the role of being his reality check. Although his management style means that you can share your opinion, and he does listen. He makes me feel valued and has supported me to form my own ideas. Sometimes I don't think he understands what it is to be an immigrant in Britain and how much courage is needed to speak to your boss. It has taken me 20 years to speak up.

'When Andrew announced he was selling the Belsize Park store, our colleague Seelan asked whether this meant that bringing the heart into business didn't work. I told Seelan that the very fact that he was standing up and asking this question meant that it did work. Seelan also comes from Sri Lanka. It's not in our culture to question the boss, especially the white man. And yet Andrew has created a culture in which we've found our voice, where we're not frightened about losing our job if we challenge our boss. Andrew put things into practice rather than just talking about it. He realised how an immigrant workforce is different. One really good thing about him is that he can admit to making a mistake. It makes a big difference that he doesn't need to be right.

'I've also never met anyone as generous as Andrew. When he sold the Belsize Park store, he gave his staff bonuses. He didn't need to do this. He makes me want to do a better job. He has always been passionate about the environment and local community, and this has led me to become passionate too.'

I was lost for words when I first read what Shanthy had said. I was both humbled and ashamed. Ashamed that, up to that point, I'd not seen how I, as the 'white man', had so impacted her life and that of so many others like her. We decided to check this out with some of the others in the team. For the non-white team members we spoke to, there were similar feelings, although it did vary by individual. One said: 'I can feel if they respect me, and if they do, I will share – if not, I shut down and stay quiet.' The issue of elders came up a lot – as the boss, I was considered an elder. And while the issue of the 'white man' becomes a bit diluted with the second generation (raised in the UK), that elder respect remained just as strong. They also raised the fact that English is not their first language. The question was: 'Can I express what I want without it being misunderstood?' If in doubt, they tend to say nothing. Talking about your emotions and feelings is tough enough at the best of times – and if you have to do this in a language you're not confident you can speak well, that's another hurdle to overcome – I can't imagine having this type of dialogue in German and wonder whether I'll ever be able to.

Most business leaders are white, middle-class men. So, if that's you, I'm urging you to fully engage with everyone in your workforce. This is a challenge facing businesses worldwide and one that I believe can be overcome by opening your heart. And while I'm delighted that so many immigrants, women and people of colour have had the chance to progress and develop at Thornton's Budgens, this is the exception rather than the rule in most businesses. But Shanthy's perspective further reinforces the fact that, if this approach can work in a multicultural supermarket in London, it can work anywhere.

Tools to help you hone your Authentic Leadership skills

Both Eudora and I have picked up many tools along the way that can help you hone your Authentic Leadership skills. Here are some of our favourites.

Tool 1: Dealing with difficult conversations

Difficult conversations are challenging to deal with at home and at work. How do I speak to someone without them getting upset/hurt/angry? In my experience, not saying anything leads to more hurt in the long term, as it all leaks out sideways. While the dislike of difficult conversations is universal, some cultures and individuals find it less of an issue. In my experience, Germans and Iranians struggle with the British/Irish beating-around-the-bush way of speaking. The reason difficult conversations are so hard is that most of us don't like confrontation, so we avoid it – until it all becomes too much and bursts out.

One of the first people to look at this topic was Marshall Rosenberg, the creator of nonviolent communication (NVC). He saw that, in charged situations, what actually happened (the data), things that happened in the past, how you feel and what you want, all get jumbled together – and, understandably, you don't get the desired outcome. When you have a tricky situation with someone, it more than likely triggers something from your past (see Chapter 3) – but if that person said or did the same thing to someone else, it would probably not have affected them in the same way.

The great thing about NVC is that it helps you to understand your feelings and own them. While you can ask someone else to change their behaviour, the only behavioural change you're in charge of is your own. So, by understanding why you find something so upsetting, you can become clearer and cleaner about communicating the impact it's having on you. Eudora and I used NVC for a number of years, with some success. However, we found it hard to master and use effectively. In search of alternatives, Eudora discovered a model called the 5 Fields authentic communication framework, developed by shadow worker Marianne Hill.

I'll use the example of an employee, Margaret, who didn't get a promotion. It's a fairly straightforward process. Capture the information that fits in each of the fields, then use that information to share with the person you're triggered by. You can use this tool in three different ways: with someone who understands the process and is able to work through the steps with you; with someone (such as your accountability buddy) standing in as a proxy for the person you are triggered by, and to help you get clear about what's going on for you. For example, Margaret could do this with a friend acting as her boss. Finally, if the other person doesn't understand or want to follow the process, you can still use it to structure how you communicate with them so that your approach is clear and clean. Here are the stages:

1. **Facts:** State the facts as if the event had been filmed on video. You can only report what happened, not how you feel. So, in our example, Margaret might say: 'The new role of sales development manager was advertised, and you were in charge of the recruitment process. I applied, as did a number of other people, including Mary. We were all interviewed, and you chose Mary for the role. When sharing the decision with me, you said Mary was the better candidate.' Clear, concise and factual.

2. **Fears and fantasies:** This is your chance to go crazy with all those thoughts inside your head. Margaret's might be: 'My fears and fantasies are that you think I'm a useless person and very disorganised, that you always favour Mary over me, and I knew you were going to choose her – that no matter how hard I try, it's never enough for you. In fact, you're impossible to please and I'm doomed to failure as long as I'm working for you.' Because this is labelled as fears and fantasies it's much easier for Margaret's boss to hear, as she isn't accusing them of anything, she's just saying what she fears. Later, the boss can share whether they really do feel she's useless. Also, the boss has helped to trigger Margaret by not giving any reason for her not getting the job, allowing her imagination to run wild.

3. **Feelings:** What are you feeling out of the five primary emotions – sadness, joy, anger, fear and shame? So, Margaret might say: 'I feel real anger about what happened – and beneath that lots of sadness that I'll never be good enough; and some shame that you think I'm not good enough.'

4. **Fortress:** This is what you're not OK about and where you feel the need to protect yourself. Margaret might say: 'I'm not OK that you promoted Mary without explaining why

she got the job and I didn't.' In fact, what Margaret has now realised is that it's not the lack of promotion she's upset about, it's the not knowing why and therefore the assumptions she has made.

5. **Forward from here:** What would help to resolve the situation? Margaret might say: 'What I'd like you to do is explain in detail why Mary got promoted and not me. I'd like to know what I need to do to have a better chance of promotion when the next opportunity arises. And I'd like us to sit down at a time that suits you to go through this in detail. Can we agree on a time before we conclude this meeting?' This is really clear, detailed and hard for the boss to say no to.

At this stage, the boss gets the chance to respond. First of all, they can play back what they heard using active listening (see Chapter 6). Then they can comment on her fears and fantasies: 'Margaret, I don't think you are useless. If I did, I wouldn't have suggested you apply for the role. I really appreciate what you bring to the team and want you to know it was a really tough decision.' They should also play back Margaret's feelings, her fortress and her request – and hopefully get their diary out to agree a time to do this. It's possible that some of Margaret's fears and fantasies are correct – i.e. that her boss does think she's disorganised. If that's the case, then it's best to have it out on the table so that action can be taken. The chances are that Margaret will learn she's not useless, just a bit disorganised (and can do something about this); what her positive characteristics are; and maybe have identified a path to promotion. Perhaps she's better suited to a creative role where being disorganised might not hold her back.

> YOUR TURN: *If you have an accountability buddy, get together and practise this – but start small. It's easier to start with a situation your buddy is not involved with. Find a charged situation with someone else in your life and have them play*

> *proxy for that person. And then switch and do the same for them. Having played with the tool this way, then see if there is something that your buddy has triggered in you. Maybe you had agreed to meet last week to discuss something, and they didn't show up. Use the 5 Fields to work through this and then ask them to do the same with you.*

If you don't have anyone to practise this with, then use the steps to imagine how you might approach a difficult conversation. If you were Margaret and there was no way your boss would be interested in this tool; nonetheless you could use it to prepare for a meeting about your lack of promotion. I've done this numerous times and it has always helped me to make progress. It certainly beats an angry outburst. Eudora and I have an agreement to follow this process when we have a difficult situation to deal with, but it's really hard in the heat of the moment when one or both of us are triggered.

There was an 18-month period at Thornton's Budgens where, following the retirement of our long-standing store manager and before the promotion of two of the team as co-leaders, I appointed an external head coach and team leader. Daniel was trained in using NVC and was on the ground every day, so he could spot situations occurring and either he or I could facilitate an NVC session. The sessions I facilitated were powerful and led to great insight and healing.

In mid-2019, Surma and Kate took over as co-leaders and I discovered the 5 Fields a few months later. My immediate thought was to train everyone to use the process. However, Kate and Surma quite rightly asked for a period to settle in and establish themselves as leaders before we set off on any new adventures. We agreed a plan to train a few people at the store as 5 Fields facilitators so they could start to help others have difficult conversations and get people comfortable with the idea. The plan was overtaken by Covid – and the rest is history. Having a number of trained 5 Fields facilitators is still, in my view, the best way to have this widely adopted in an organisation. If you agree, then do let me know as maybe yours could become the laboratory.

Tool 2: Appreciation

Appreciation is one of the keys to opening your heart. Due to the brain's negative bias, we're always on the alert for negative comments, so it's refreshing (and sometimes a bit difficult) to hear positive remarks. I spend my whole day looking for opportunities to appreciate people, be they colleagues, family, friends, a waiter or someone serving me in a shop or the gas man who came out late on a freezing winter evening. And it is extraordinary how little appreciation most people receive in their jobs and how it can lift someone.

Until it feels natural, leave yourself reminders – maybe a Post-it note on your laptop or add it to the reminders app on your phone. And when you're sharing appreciation with someone, make sure you do it descriptively. I learnt this concept from parenting coach Noël Janis-Norton. It's about delivering specific and detailed compliments. It isn't enough to say: 'Bob, you're amazing.' Whether he's your five-year-old son, your partner or your direct report, Bob has probably heard enough negative feedback from you to render that claim dubious.

You can start to shift that negative bias in the following ways. To the five-year-old, you could say: 'Bob, I love that drawing you've done and the way you've used so many different colours. I can really imagine I'm on that beach you've drawn.' To your partner, you might say: 'Bob, I really appreciated that dinner you cooked for my birthday. Even though there was a lot of tricky stuff going on between us and you were unwell, you produced a really delicious meal and I felt really celebrated.' And to your direct report: 'Bob, I really appreciated how, despite all the pressure you're under producing the year-end financial results, that you were prepared to give me your time when I said I needed your help with a legal issue.'

Remember to appreciate yourself descriptively too, as this will help to neutralise the voice of your inner critic. Also, make sure you listen when other people appreciate you and, if necessary, repeat it back to yourself afterwards. If you think that all this talking to yourself is a bit crazy, just be aware that inside your mind you spend a huge amount of time talking to yourself, and studies have shown most of that talk is negative. It's your job to counter this.

> YOUR TURN: *This is a great exercise you can do in a team meeting or any other gathering, such as an awayday or training workshop, where you have a group of people that know each other or have just got to know each other. Sitting in a circle, get one person to volunteer. The person to their left then shares with them and the group (in a sentence or two) one thing that they appreciate about that volunteer. You then go clockwise, with each person in the group telling the volunteer what they appreciate about them. When the circle is complete, move clockwise to the next person – and repeat the process.*

Given that people often find it hard to hear or absorb appreciation, when we do this exercise, we record each round on a WhatsApp message and send it to the person being appreciated so they can listen to it later. It's amazing how powerful and healing this process can be. However, there are some people for whom it's almost impossible to hear appreciation. If you're going to do an exercise like the one above, you need to allow people to leave the room when it's their turn. You can then record the appreciation and encourage them to listen to it later.

In many companies the traditional appraisal process places its focus on developmental needs rather than what you excel at. Shanthy told me that she had kept a copy of the first appraisal I gave her almost 30 years ago, when I was very much the profit-focused entrepreneur. She has shared enough of it for me to get a sense of how tough I was and how demotivating it must've been for her at the time. Nowadays I look for things that are working and share that positive feedback with colleagues. At Thornton's Budgens, we started our leadership meetings with a round of what was going well to get the meeting off to a positive start rather than diving straight into the issues of the day.

Appreciation is one of the habits we used to anchor behaviours at Thornton's Budgens (see Chapter 8), so I was extremely gratified when I read Jahid's interview, which you can read at the end of this chapter. He believes that appreciation is more valuable than money – and I agree.

Tool 3: Gratitude

I place a lot of importance on gratitude. To support this and help me live as much as I can from a place of gratitude, I do a nightly exercise adapted from a practice called the Examen Prayer, developed by St Ignatius, founder of the Jesuits. Every evening before I go to bed, I review my day and what I'm grateful for. I know that, even if I felt I had a rubbish day, I can find a number of things to be grateful for. Right now, it's the sun pouring through the window on this Irish winter's day; the walk and swim on the beach with my sister; finding a nice big puddle beside a clump of grass to clean off the dog poo I had trodden in (and focusing on that rather than being angry about the dog poo in the first place); and a couple of conversations with Eudora, who's at home in Germany. I've recently added two more dimensions – something I learnt today and something that delighted me today.

All the science shows that our brains are the same as our muscles – if we exercise the gratitude part of our brain, it'll grow stronger, just like our legs will with running. If we exercise the 'my life is rubbish' muscles, they too will grow strong. And I know which brain muscles I want to be working out. As researcher and author Brené Brown says: 'A good life happens when you stop and are grateful for the ordinary moments that so many of us just steamroll over to try to find those extraordinary moments.'

Tool 4: Humour

It's scientifically proven that laughing is good for our mental health and wellbeing – and, in my experience, we generally don't do enough of it in the workplace. My colleague Vanessa is a facilitator and artist and has produced a set of Be the Change cards. We often use them at workshops and it's extraordinary how relevant a seemingly randomly chosen card can be. Recently, I've started to draw one at the beginning of the day to give me some insight. And guess what? The card I drew this morning was about silliness! In the guidebook, Vanessa wrote about this card:

Too much logic
My brain needs a break!
Can't take this now
Please give me a shake!
Wobble me out of here
Sideways, undressed
Upside down too
Then I'll be at my best!

In our workshops, we always try to bring in humour to lighten things up and shake creativity into action. At work, I'm not so sure I'm as good at this but am making progress. When I moved in with Eudora, Hanne said she wanted to have a talk with me. Her words were along the lines of: 'Andrew, you're way too serious. If we're going to get along, you're going to have to lighten up.' She was six at the time! We agreed that she'd be my 'silly clown trainer' and it has gone pretty well over the past five years.

After my 18 months as a graduate trainee at Mars, I was promoted to a role called sales research manager. I inherited a team of five people, including Ian and Nigel, both of whom had a great sense of fun. We had a great time while doing some amazingly cutting-edge and creative work. The view then was that we got away with things others would not because our work was so good. I now see it was the other way round – our good work came from our sense of fun. So, on your journey to opening your and other people's hearts, have some fun, be silly and laugh at every opportunity – I guarantee it'll lead to great things.

Tool 5: Journaling

Writing is a powerful way of helping to clear your mind and allow new ideas to emerge. Prior to learning NVC, if I was really angry with someone, I would write them an email that let it all out – and then not send it. It's amazing how refreshing and releasing this felt. These days, if it's someone I want an ongoing relationship with, I'd use all of my tools to address the situation. If you're angry with someone you aren't in a relationship with anymore, or they're dead, writing them a letter and burning it can be transformative. Every morning, before my meditation, I do a few minutes of journaling – it helps me acknowledge things that are going on inside my head and clears some of them out.

> YOUR TURN: *Take out your journal and write for five minutes without stopping. Write whatever wants to come out – don't edit it and remember that no one else is going to read it so you can be totally free. How did you feel afterwards? If you find this helpful, build it into your daily routine.*

A word about habits

A habit is defined in the *Oxford Dictionary of English* as 'a settled or regular tendency or practice, especially one that is hard to give up'. The process of becoming an Authentic Leader requires you to become aware of unhelpful habits and let them go, while at the same time developing new habits that will help you become more authentically yourself. Being a good boy and taking on too much work as you're afraid your money will run out are two examples of 'hard to give up' habits that might hinder your ability to be truly authentic, whereas appreciation and having difficult conversations are habits you could develop to help you thrive.

The same approach applies to organisations, and in Chapter 8 you'll see how we used the idea of habits as part of Thornton's Budgens' manifesto. However, there's one particular habit that I believe every business would benefit from developing: being on the pitch. I first came across this idea at the Landmark Forum. They used the analogy of a football game – there are 22 players on the pitch and a referee, with thousands in the stands watching and maybe hundreds of thousands watching on TV. The men or women on the pitch are risking it all and putting so much of themselves into the game. Many in the stands (or their armchairs) will enjoy the game and also indulge in being the critic. It's easy to criticise from the stands – the players on the pitch are the ones putting themselves out there.

In your life, be that at work, with your family, with your hobbies – are you on the pitch putting yourself out there, or are you sitting in the wings criticising those on the pitch? As you'll see in our manifesto, 'Being on the pitch and not in the stands' is one of Thornton's Budgens' habits. What that means is that everyone is encouraged to take responsibility. In our weekly operations meeting, the deli manager could take one of two approaches. He could say: 'I'm aware that the sales in my area are down and we need to do something. I'm not sure what the issue is, and I'd love your help in coming up with some ideas.' Or he could say: 'Yes, I know sales are down – Fred and Mary aren't up to the job and now that Morrisons also has a deli, what can we do?' Can you feel the difference? Which version do you think will help shift something?

YOUR TURN: *Pick a work or personal situation where you can admit to being in the stands and decide to get on the pitch. See how things shift – how does it feel? Do things get resolved more easily and quickly?*

Self-care for the Authentic Leader

If you're going to be an open-hearted Authentic Leader, you need to take care of yourself. As an adult, you're 100 per cent responsible for yourself (and your children, if you have them), and if you don't take care of yourself, no one else will. There are thousands of self-care books out there and I've read a few in my time. We all have different needs, but I hope that by sharing what works for me, I might tempt you to discover what works for you.

The idea of self-care was an eye-opener for many at Thornton's Budgens. One team member, who was originally from a village in Bangladesh, told Eudora: 'I have learnt that self-care is essential. If I give myself permission to take time out for myself and have a rest, then it's much easier for me to be present and be there for other people. Having a rest after work helps me approach my housework with a cool mindset.' Notice how she says that when she takes care of herself, she can be more present, and being present is one of the key principles of being an Authentic Leader. There are four key areas of self-care – food and drink, sleep, physical exercise and mental wellbeing.

Key area 1: Food and drink

Soaring levels of childhood and adult obesity demonstrate that we're currently in a food and drink crisis. Our bodies need fuel and what we eat and drink provides that fuel. However, if we consume the wrong fuel, we're not going to function very well – it's like putting diesel in a petrol engine. Over the years I've tried gluten-free, dairy-free and carb-free diets. In 2020, Eudora and I set out to do Veganuary. The fact that we postponed the start until 5th January wasn't a good sign – and it was hard. Other than finding a few excellent vegan restaurants in London, as the household chef I found it tough to produce vegan meals that all three of us enjoyed. I was particularly busy at work and didn't have the time or energy to reinvent my approach to the kitchen. A lot of what I served up was politely (and sometimes less than politely) declined! We lasted about two weeks.

After my adrenal fatigue diagnosis, both Eudora and her ex-husband gave me a copy of the book *How Not to Die*, by Dr Michael Greger. He goes through all of the main killer diseases of the Western world and concludes that the cure for each and every one is the same – a plant-based diet. The breakthrough for me was when he said you don't have to become a vegan, just cut down on your consumption of meat and dairy. I also had some further motivation to change. Shortly before my diagnosis, I had an unexpectedly high prostate-specific antigen (PSA) score. I had an MRI, and while the consultant was fairly confident it wasn't cancer, it felt like an early warning. Being off work while recovering from adrenal fatigue also helped, in that my primary task of the day was to buy and cook food for the family, so I had the time to experiment and create a whole new range of dishes. My diet is now about 75 per cent plant based. We rarely eat meat at home, leaving that for special occasions. I can still have my beloved butter and occasional cheese, and have found some great-tasting non-dairy yoghurts and milks, and even a few cheeses. I definitely feel better, and a number of my health measures (e.g. cholesterol) have shifted in a positive direction. When I went back to see the oncologist after just four months on the 75 per cent vegan diet, my PSA score had more than halved.

With drink, most of what I have read recommends that we should drink plenty of water – so I do. There are times when I forget, but as soon as I remember, I can feel my body rehydrating and responding joyfully to that lubrication. Regarding alcohol, there's no doubt that too much is bad for you. When I started to meditate regularly about 10 years ago, I noticed a gradual reduction in my tolerance for alcohol. As I was becoming more sensitive to the needs of my body, it was speaking back to me and telling me not to overdo it. Adrenal fatigue further reduced my tolerance, so now I need to keep listening to my body, even though my beloved red wine has become an occasional treat.

Key area 2: Sleep

Another pivotal book for me was *Why We Sleep* by Matthew Walker. It's packed with study after study about the impact of sleep, or lack thereof. He shares studies that show that a lack of sleep reduces life expectancy, contributes to dementia, and that most of us need eight hours' sleep a night, every night. He believes that missing sleep during the week and catching up at the weekend doesn't work. I know that my cumulative lack of sleep, which built up over years and years, was the single biggest contributor to my adrenal fatigue. And while getting enough sleep was easier while I was off work recovering, as I returned to work, I had to totally change my way of being. Here are some of the techniques I have experimented with:

- ❤ I undertook a programme at the Optimum Health Clinic in London, which helped me to focus on how overstimulated I was and how to reduce that stimulation.

- ❤ With the support of a nutritionist at the Optimum Health Clinic, I take various supplements to help calm my system and recently added a few that a friend in the US recommended, which have transformed my ability to sleep.

- ❤ I've increased my awareness of when my mind is racing and use breathing exercises (see Wim Hof, below) to help slow it down.

- ❤ I take regular breaks from work, with a daily 15-minute period when I listen to relaxing instrumental music.

- ❤ I walk more slowly and rush less, which means getting to appointments super early rather than leaving it until the last minute.

- ❤ I switch off my phone and all other electronic devices no later than 9 pm, preferably earlier.

- ❤ I stick to a regular bedtime, no later than 10 pm.

- ❤ I do a ten-minute yoga routine followed by a hot bath before going to bed.

- ❤ I work fewer hours and have more time outside in nature, particularly walking and outdoor swimming.

- ❤ I practise mindfulness, as a whirring mind is one of the things that stops me sleeping at night.

I've avoided sleeping pills, as I know a few people who are now addicted to them. They can work, but I believe many of the medications people take are covering up what their bodies are trying to tell them. Mine was yelling at me to slow down!

Based on what I found to work for me, some of these practices are now part of my daily routine and have become habits, so I now almost always have eight hours' sleep a night. My situation was extreme and the adrenal fatigue was my body telling me that there were aspects of my life that I loved (like late nights fuelled by red wine) that would have to go – sad, and the reality of what my body needs at this moment.

Be honest with yourself – do you really get enough sleep? If the answer is no, I encourage you to try some of the above and read Matthew Walker's book. You might say: 'That's all very well for you, but I have my boss breathing down my neck 24/7, I don't have time to do any of this stuff.' This may be true now and, if it is, ask yourself is that really how you want to live your life? I believe that, as we move forward, more and more businesses are going to have to prioritise their employees' physical and mental wellbeing, so maybe it's time for you to find one that does.

Key area 3: Exercise

I have no doubt that staying physically fit is one of the keys to a long and fulfilling life. My maternal grandfather is my role model. He walked for at least an hour a day every day of his life and at least two hours a day when he retired. When he had a massive heart attack in his early 80s, he was initially told he was too old for any type of treatment until they realised what good shape he was in. They gave his heart a good 'service' and he enjoyed a new lease of life. He eventually died when he was almost 90.

I know that a healthy body leads to a healthy mind. I know that if I stop work in the middle of the day for a walk, run or swim, I'll end up getting more done and being more effective, even though I'll spend fewer hours actually working. As with food, this is personal. You need to find what works for you and which form of exercise gives you pleasure. I don't subscribe to the 'no pain, no gain' mantra. For me, that means running, cycling (I don't own a car in London so the bike is my main form of transport), walking, swimming and skiing when I can. One of the attractions of our home in Germany is that it's on the edge of the Alps, so I can easily get to a ski hill in under an hour and ski cross-country from my front door.

I also swim outdoors all year round. In London it's Hampstead Ponds; in Germany it's the local river or lake. I'm writing this chapter in my native Dublin by the Irish Sea, and I've been swimming every day I've been here. I feel so much more alive after a winter swim and there are many benefits. A friend reported not getting regular winter colds when he took up outdoor swimming (I have found the same) and a good friend, who suffers from a mood disorder, knows her mood will be lifted if she swims outdoors. If this appeals to you, explore the work of the exuberant Dutchman Wim Hof, who promotes the benefits of taking a two-minute cold shower daily (which I do) and sitting in iced water tubs (which I haven't tried yet). He has also developed breathing exercises and has researched and proven the benefits of all of this for good physical and mental wellbeing.

Many of us spend way too little time moving and too much time hunched over a keyboard. If you're holding meetings (or online calls) that last longer than an hour, I recommend that you get everyone to stand up and do some movement – stretching, star jumps, dancing, whatever. The other thing you can do during a long meeting is to get people to change places a few times. This literally helps people to see things from a different perspective and keeps up the energy levels.

> YOUR TURN: *Next time you are holding a meeting that's going to last for more than an hour, take two minutes halfway through to do some physical movement and then get everyone to move to a different seat. Notice how it energises the meeting.*

Key area 4: Mental wellbeing

This is a huge subject, so I'll just share what has worked for me. Scientific evidence supports the benefits of meditation and mindfulness as a route to a happier, healthier life. One study that I read many years ago really struck me. It correlated the number of hours (in their lifetime) that participants had meditated and how they reacted or responded to situations presented to them. A reaction is instant and often disproportionate, while a response is made after a split-second pause. The study showed that the more meditation someone had done, the longer the pause before taking action. This pause is awareness and gives you the chance to choose how you respond to a given situation. I've meditated for 15–20 minutes every morning reasonably consistently for over 10 years. I don't sit there like a monk in Zen pose – my mind flies around all over the place and I have to keep bringing it back to stillness. It's hard at times, very tempting to skip, yet I feel confident that it brings a sense of calm and improves my ability to pause and respond rather than react.

Eudora compares meditation to maintaining a car. 'It's important to make sure your car goes in for its yearly service, that the oil is regularly checked, that the car is cleaned and there's enough petrol in the tank. If your car is in good order, then you can respond more efficiently to those many unexpected emergencies that life throws at you. Practising meditation and taking time to reflect keeps your heart, body and mind connected so that you can respond appropriately to the adventures of life.'

The importance of awareness

This plays a huge part in Authentic Leadership. With awareness you can be much more present with what you're doing, and as a result have more choices regarding how you respond to any given situation. Presence is really important in business, and especially so in retail. On the shop floor you're 'on duty' for customers at all times.

Eudora recently had an experience that illustrates this perfectly. She visited our local stationery shop (where she is a regular customer) to look for a new fountain pen. It took some time to attract a shop assistant's attention, but finally they gave her some pens to try out. The assistant was interrupted by another customer and started to serve them, abandoning Eudora. This happened a couple of times and Eudora eventually left. A few days later, she tried a different store. They were fully attentive the whole time, which she really appreciated. She ended up spending more than €100 on two fountain pens and some school supplies for Hanne, and will never return to the original shop, which has now lost her as a customer due to one team member's lack of presence and awareness. In the retail and hospitality industries, I have a simple mantra – presence delivers exceptional service.

This applies just as much outside of retail. Think of a moment when a colleague approached you with a question. Did you carry on typing while half-listening? Or did you stop what you're doing and give them your full attention? You could also choose to say that you're focused on something else right now and agree on an (acceptable) time when you can give them your full attention.

The Authentic Leadership approach has a positive impact on all aspects of people's lives, not just their work. As Jahid points out in the following interview, so many of the team at Thornton's Budgens have experienced huge benefits that have impacted their family's lives as well as their communities.

Thornton's Budgens team interview #3

Name: Jahid Chowdhury
Nationality: Asian British, born in Bangladesh
Position: Team leader
Length of service: 15 years

I was given a lot of responsibility from an early age. At 21 I was a partner in my own business and had been made chairman of the mosque. I took my responsibilities seriously and tried to do my best for the people I led. I came to England in August 2005, and a few months later started working at Thornton's Budgens. During my time there, I have seen real changes in the leadership style. Initially Jim was in charge, and everything went through him. Over time there was more of a structure, with managers and organisational layers.

Andrew started to develop a coaching culture. My potential was recognised, and I was promoted. Initially the new culture was confusing, but over the course of two years I learnt about coaching and found it amazing. I started to understand what putting the heart back into business meant. I realised that positive thinking means you can overcome anything. Positive people can change the world. The two-year coaching programme changed me completely. Previously I would jump to anger when I discovered that a member of staff had forgotten to do something or not done their job properly. After the coaching programme, I'd take a deep breath and approach the situation in a calm and patient manner. This created a new type of relationship with my team as well as my family. I have always been close to my wife and now she really appreciates my calm and patient manner.

The coaching motivated me to do things differently. I learnt to be more open minded and take on more responsibility. I realised that I could help people grow. Then Thornton's Budgens started to explore shared leadership, which creates a clean and safe working environment. It's important to have a balance between a clear leadership structure and the freedom to allow people to think outside the box.

I feel happy and fulfilled at work. I never feel as if I'll lose my job. I'm involved with every new decision and value the frequent appreciation I receive, not only from Andrew but also from the other leaders. I believe that appreciation is more valuable than money.

 **5**

Organisational Purpose

Now that you're well on your way to becoming an Authentic Leader, let's move on to organisational purpose. I believe it's almost impossible to be effective and fulfilled in a job where your personal purpose does not align with that of the organisation you work for. If you can link personal purpose and organisational purpose, it can be really powerful. If you discover that your purpose doesn't align with your employer's, you can choose to move on. And for the employer, it isn't helpful to have team members who aren't in alignment with the organisation's purpose; the more senior the person, the more of an issue it becomes.

Aileen Richards told me: 'I stayed at Mars for 30 years, as I had a very good values match with the company – and that's absolutely critical. Mars and I have a fundamental belief that businesses have huge potential and indeed a responsibility to be a force for good in society. I felt I could make more impact, in terms of making the world a better place, by staying in an organisation that believed we had to stand up and do good in society, as other players were not always willing or able to do that.'

A few years ago, I was invited to visit a retailer by their CEO, who liked the idea of our heart work and was curious about how it could be applied. The business had a great purpose and set of values (on paper), but these weren't coming alive across the business. The HR director felt that they needed to 're-induct' the organisation in their purpose and values. As part of the day I spent with them, I met numerous employees, visited a number of their stores and spent time with half the board. I vividly remember sitting with the finance director, whose view was that the problem lay with the HR and marketing departments. He felt that if the HR department properly communicated their values, then the employees would behave differently; and that if the marketing department communicated these values to their customers they would buy more, and all would be good. His job was just to do the numbers.

I also had a similar conversation with a second director. I discovered that these two directors didn't connect with the purpose and values of the organisation and felt it wasn't their job to be involved or care about them. I shared with the CEO, maybe too bluntly, that until all of his board were aligned on their purpose and values, they could communicate and induct to their heart's content, and they'd get nowhere. And given the intransigence of the two aforementioned directors, in all likelihood he'd have to move them on anyway. We parted on good terms, but I never heard from him again. At the time, I wondered if I'd made a mistake and been too blunt. Since then, I've become more and more certain about the need to be authentic. I'm certain that I did the right thing and that the CEO and the organisation were not ready to change.

The role of organisational purpose

Reading a book about marketing recently, I was struck by the author's view that the reason organisations existed was 'for selling or effecting transactions'. Sadly, that's how many companies see it – and no matter how much they dress it up, that's it: it's transactional and about money. In his excellent (and similarly titled) book, *The Heart of Business,* Hubert Joly (who saved Best Buy in the US from its predicted demise) traced this view back to Milton Friedman and stated that, contrary to Friedman's view, 'the purpose of a company is not to make money, but rather to contribute to the common good and serve all its stakeholders'. He went on to say that 'corporations are not soulless entities, but human organisations with people at their centre, working together in support of that purpose'.

Companies consist of groups of people, and people need meaning in their lives. This purpose can be a complete dedication to meeting the needs of its customers, as was the case with Tesco before the balance moved towards profit being its purpose. That shift at Tesco led to the Serious Fraud Office being called in and subsequently a massive loss in shareholder value. And although many businesses are jumping on the purpose bandwagon (and in my view not all of them are being authentic), the idea of business having a purpose beyond maximising shareholder value is in the ascendancy.

Rita Clifton shares my optimism: 'I've been banging my head against a wall and getting strange looks since the mid-Eighties. Now I have people in business saying how important the environment is. My response is, "No shit, Sherlock! It's happening!" Renewed organisations like Tesco and Unilever are doing really well, as are businesses that have always had purpose at their heart, like Patagonia. I love helping leaders realise their people will be happier, their customers will feel warmer towards them, and they'll create a lower-risk, higher-return business if they take a longer-term view.'

Like me, she's encouraged by the likes of Larry Fink, CEO of investment management firm BlackRock, who thinks that companies also need to show how they can make a positive contribution to society.

One of my all-time favourite mission statements was the one created for Apple by Steve Jobs: 'To make a contribution to the world by making tools for the mind that advance humankind.' I don't know about you, but I'd certainly have been motivated by this purpose. The opposite of that is the 'let's make as much cash as possible' type of purpose. While it might be desirable to have everyone focused on 'making tools for the mind that advance humankind', if a similar focus is placed on making money, I believe it can, and eventually will, go awry. It's also worth noting that, without a clear, written purpose, an informal unconscious and unspoken one emerges, which is often about increasing profits. Few businesses are bold enough to state that their purpose is about generating cash – they just act that way. I believe that a clear purpose needs to unite all stakeholders behind something that will become the organisation's entire focus, so a culture can be created that aligns with that purpose. To work, a purpose has to be authentic and lived. I believe that customers and employees can sense when it's fake. Patagonia is one of the most purposeful companies in the world. Founded in 1973 by Yvon Chouinard, their mission is 'to build the best product, cause no unnecessary harm, and use business to inspire and implement solutions to address issues related to the environment and social justice'. Even in 1973, he saw the need to address the climate crisis. Everything they do is lined up behind and defined by this purpose – and it's truly authentic.

In *The Heart of Business*, Hubert Joly described the process he and his colleagues at Best Buy went through to develop what he called their 'noble' purpose, which was 'to enrich our customers' lives through technology' – and that they would do this through addressing their human needs in areas such as entertainment, productivity, communication, food, security, and health and wellness.

Rita Clifton shared her experiences of doing this at Nationwide (a UK building society), where she is now a NED. She said that, when she joined, they were seen as a bit different from other financial institutions, but not that much different, considering they were owned by their members. She discovered that they operated in silos and didn't really take advantage of their mutuality. Having looked at other mutuals such as John Lewis and BUPA, they realised that their purpose was staring them in the face: 'Building society nationwide.' She said: 'Nationwide generally runs its purpose as an organising principle behind how it prioritises ideas, how it looks after its members, its employees and the role it plays in the community, and that's now extended into funding a new housing development in Swindon with a strong social purpose behind what sort of community they want to create.'

And finally, Aileen Richards told me that there's a famous letter written by Forrest Mars Snr in 1947 that says: 'The sole purpose of Mars is to provide a mutuality of benefits for all its stakeholders', which was an extremely sophisticated concept for its time, just after the Second World War.

Disconnection from your organisational purpose

The other side of the coin is either not having a purpose or being disconnected from it. As I mentioned earlier, in the 2010s, Tesco got into difficulties. As one of the world's largest grocers, they are a dominant player in the market I've spent a lot of my life operating in. However, after decades of success, things started to go off track. Did an excessive focus on profits lead to this? Was it the same pressure that led to the Dieselgate scandal at German car maker Volkswagen, where they systematically fiddled emissions tests? Did that same profit pressure lead BP to cut safety corners, leading to the Deep Water Horizon oil rig disaster, the loss of 11 lives and the destruction of an ecosystem in the Gulf of Mexico? In an even more extreme situation, the enquiry into the 2017 Grenfell Tower fire in London found that, rather than putting safety first, the manufacturer of the cladding had faked the safety tests. Having failed the first one, they used a superior material for the second, but continued to sell the cheaper (and less safe) version) as 'certified'.

The result was an inferno as a result of which 72 people died. All four of these situations are examples of what can happen when you focus excessively on profits – a drive generally justified by the need to maximise shareholder value. Unfortunately, in each case, it led to the exact opposite – a huge loss in shareholder value and, in some cases, a loss of life.

I was always fascinated by Tesco and, for many years, observed them from a distance. Thanks initially to Budgens' brand owner Booker merging with Tesco, and then from our work on plastics (see Chapter 9), I got to know Dave Lewis, who was Tesco CEO from 2014 to 2020. After his departure, I had the chance to interview him about what went wrong prior to his arrival and what he did to address their issues.

'In a way, Tesco became a victim of its own success,' Dave told me. 'There was a very strong "customer champion" mindset along with one of the most efficient store-operating models in the world, which was expanded by buying and building more stores. That combination was very successful for a very long period of time and made Tesco one of the most profitable retailers in the world. As a result, there was a financial delivery that was above market average, close to 6 per cent at its peak. Then growth began to slow, so the financial model came under pressure. Tesco was at its best when it was championing the customer and a nice financial number popped out at the bottom. However, when the question became about how to keep the financial delivery when growth slowed down, the business lost its focus on customers and started to increase pressure on suppliers to preserve the financial position. The customer went from being all dominating and central, to finance becoming central and all dominating. An operating margin of 5.2 per cent was the only target. So, you start to cut corners and you start to have a problem – the world-class operating machinery that had been serving customers all that time starts to serve a different goal and starts to chew itself up. There is obviously a market influence – it's a function of how that business is judged, and people are judged by the City. Keeping up the dividend flow, the credit rating, everything that was seen to be critical to the share price became dominant. This process, which took place over a number of years, left a huge pressure within the business to deliver the numbers – and to me, their unwritten purpose became the 5.2 per cent margin. People were pushed to their limit in this sole focus on the delivery of the numbers. So much so that a particular team started to book supplier payments ahead of time – which is illegal – and the Serious Fraud Office ended up being called in.'

By then the CEO had been fired, there was a huge loss in shareholder value as the share price crashed, and Dave had been recruited to turn things around. Everything the business had been doing was about preserving the share price and yet that's what got hammered. This to me is the extreme version of a business being focused on the numbers and not a meaningful purpose. So, here's a question for you – have you ever experienced anything like that, maybe not so extreme, but similar in some way? How was it? Did you feel motivated and enthusiastic about going to work – or drained and worn out?

Purpose must drive everything you do

A clear purpose needs to drive everything a company does, full stop. It's the fundamental building block for any organisation. In the early days of Thornton's Budgens, we had a sense that we wanted to be a force for good, but weren't clear about how or why – and while that did not lead us to grey accounting areas, it did lead to chaos and exhaustion. In 2012, when I did my first COR leadership training programme in the US and started to develop my own purpose, the light went on – if I needed a purpose, then surely my company needed one too. It's not something I'd ever really thought about before. As it happened, at the time I'd commissioned a research company to interview customers across both stores to get some feedback on how we were doing. I joined the research lead and managers from both stores, and we locked ourselves in a hotel for a day. Our purpose emerged as: 'We are the community supermarket that cares.' Later on, we added 'about people and planet', but the essence hadn't changed, and it defined everything we did. At the same time, we also felt we needed to create some values to support the purpose. Here I made a mistake in allowing a consultant who was working with us at the time to interview me and from that produce a set of values. They looked fine, but did not connect with anyone, and even I would have struggled to recite them.

To make a difference, a set of values needs to tick a number of boxes, but our first attempt at this failed on all counts. This is what I've learnt about eliciting values:

1. They need to mean something to the people in the business. The values we came up with were not only theoretical but also developed by an external consultant. They did not mean anything to me or the team, and they needed to be relatable and actionable.

2. They have to be modelled every day by the leaders of the business. As soon as leaders stop doing this, the values become meaningless. No one in our leadership team could remember our values, let alone live them.

3. They need to be consistently communicated at every opportunity – and we failed to do this.

When I worked at Mars, their Five Principles fulfilled all of the above criteria, so it's worth checking them out on the Mars website to see how business values work in practice. As you'll see in Chapter 8, we did a much better job with our values when we came up with our manifesto.

Why your purpose needs to be authentic

Yes, your purpose must be authentic. That sounds obvious, but how often have you as a customer or supplier seen a corporate mission statement in a glossy report or up on the office wall that has made you stop and think: 'Really?'

When I discussed this with Rita Clifton, she said: 'I think that's often the challenge around purpose-led businesses. If it doesn't bubble up authentically from who you are and where you come from, what people care about and believe in, it's going to be incredibly hard for that to penetrate the organisation.' And Aileen Richards pointed out: 'It's good that, as a result of social media, the ability to "purposewash" or "greenwash" has gone – therefore authenticity and integrity have become so much more important. Not having them is much easier to sniff out – it holds people to account.' While customers will sniff out inauthenticity, the upside of this, as Rita told me, is that 'it's good, cheap marketing when you have enthusiastic customers who know what you're about and are trying to do, and are willing to tell others in an authentic way. You create a fan base that then amplifies that, rather than having to pay a lot of money to create a marketing funnel.'

We certainly benefited from many enthusiastic customers at various stages of the Thornton's Budgens journey. And, one day, one did sniff out some inauthenticity. Outside the store, the customer pointed to the purpose that was proudly written on our awning: 'If you are the community supermarket that really cares, why are you still selling sweets in your checkout queue?' I couldn't argue with him and replied that yes, that was out of sync, and we'd address it. I'd been against it for years, but experienced huge resistance internally and with Budgens' head office because of how many sweets we sold there. When we had our new purpose in place it made the action much easier to implement. There was still some resistance, but it was harder to argue with it.

Purpose requires difficult decisions

The above is an example of a business decision that had a cost for Thornton's Budgens – in the short term, we lost sales. That's why, pre-purpose, that decision hadn't been taken. Another example is the decision that Mars took in 2012 to introduce front-of-pack calorie labelling and to stop selling all single-serve packs with more than 250 calories. That meant the death of their King Size range of products, which would've accounted for many hundreds of millions of dollars in global sales. This was a bold and necessary decision to help them live their authentic purpose.

These days, almost every time I'm on a panel or being interviewed, I'm asked how businesses can avoid greenwash and have their environmental commitments taken seriously by the public. My answer is simple – have a clear and authentic purpose. In fact, I can guarantee that if you put the components of a heart-centred business in place, there's a near-zero chance of being accused of greenwash. That's why, at Thornton's Budgens, we were never accused of greenwash and why I doubt that accusation has ever been made against Patagonia.

Let's return to Tesco and what Dave Lewis discovered when he joined. One of the first things he did was plenty of listening, both directly and through internal groups: 'We rewrote the purpose that existed at that time – "We make what matters better together" – because nobody understood it or could relate to it. When asked about values, people said there are three – "Nobody tries harder for customers", "Treat people how you'd like to be treated", and a more recent one, "We use our scale for good". People said: "We really like the first two values – there's nothing wrong with them, it's just you guys that don't live them." They liked the new "scale for good" but didn't really understand it nor could they relate to it. All three values did not fit the criteria I outlined above. I wanted a purpose everyone could relate to and explained why this business existed. If you're the only person in the room and you make a decision that supports that purpose, you'll never have a problem. That's how we got to: "Serving Britain's shoppers a little better every day". We broke down every single word – e.g. to serve. People think that just means serving at the checkout and in store, but it's broader than that. If the customer knew what you knew, what would they want you to do on their behalf? That's how we got into sustainable agriculture, plastics, renewable energy, food waste, etc. On the bigger environmental issues customers will say: "I care about this, but I don't understand or know what to do in every case. Can you please take care of it for me?" It's what a responsible business would do. We kept the first two values and reinterpreted the third one to say: "Every little help can make a big difference." So what you had was a mix of two original values that were co-created with colleagues 20-plus years ago, as well as a new one.'

By the time Dave left Tesco, he says 96 per cent of people who worked for Tesco could relate to the purpose and 90 per cent could see how their job related to that purpose. Everything they did worked back from 'Serving Britain's shoppers a little better every day'. Their interpretation of service got them into their work on plastics and renewable energy – it all lined up behind their purpose.

How to develop your organisational purpose

Here are some thoughts on how to develop a purpose for your organisation:

- ❤ The leadership team must be involved in the process. If the founder is still associated with the business in any way, they need to be included; and if it's a family-run business, the family needs to be included. This is not something that can be done by committee, and it needs all the key stakeholders to be engaged. Real leadership skills are required to achieve this.

💙 It's good to have your customer at the table, as their perspective is important. It doesn't mean you can't come up with a radically new direction, but if you're going to be doing this, it's good to know that's what you're doing! With Thornton's Budgens, we'd built a base of respect for doing the right thing and customers could see this. So, our purpose wasn't a leap into something brand new, just a clarification and tightening up of what we stood for.

💙 Don't outsource your purpose to consultants. It's my guess that most glossy report mission statements are prepared by non-stakeholders and signed off by the board because they think it looks good. Recently I've been helping a food supplier with their purpose – and while initially they were keen to have my perspective on the words they were using, they eventually realised that what I thought didn't matter – it had to come from them.

💙 Do get help with facilitation. As leaders, it can be tough to see the wood for the trees, so it helps to have an objective outsider leading the process. And it's also good to have some sort of structure – to get all the views, options and opinions on the table, and then use a creative process to evolve the wording.

💙 Get yourself and your team out of your heads and into your hearts, away from the day-to-day grind. Ensure that you run any purpose sessions at an offsite venue, ideally one surrounded by nature. In helping companies to find their purpose, I've used visualisations and other techniques to open people's hearts, as that's where they instinctively know the right direction to go in.

💙 Don't rush it – it's better to do this in a number of sessions than to try and force it into an afternoon. If you develop a meaningful purpose, it should stand you in good stead for years, decades or even centuries – so there's no need to get it knocked out next week. And while the session that we ran to develop our purpose was completed in a day, we had done all of our preparation work, so what emerged resonated with everyone. Be patient and be prepared to rework it until something clicks.

To help with the development of your organisational purpose, former Best Buy CEO Hubert Joly has adapted the *ikigai* process (see Figure 1 in Chapter 2) for companies by suggesting that you can create a noble purpose by looking at the intersection of:

- 🖤 what the world needs
- 🖤 the company's capabilities
- 🖤 what drives people at the company, what they are passionate about, what they aspire to
- 🖤 how to make money.

> YOUR TURN: *Think of your organisation. Do you feel you have a clear purpose that unites all stakeholders? If yes, that's great. If not, is the time right to develop one? If so, work out a plan, ask who needs to be involved and how you're going to do this. If you can initiate this, great. If not, ask yourself who can and how you can encourage them to do so. A good start to this process could be to answer the* ikigai *questions above.*

Eudora has helped a number of companies (and individuals within those companies) develop their personal and organisational purpose: 'When a company's purpose is clear and lived on a day-to-day basis, there's a feeling of ease throughout the organisation, and individuals can then connect their personal purpose to the organisation's purpose. When this happens there's a strong sense that everyone is moving in the same direction, and this will be felt internally and externally by all stakeholders. Time is not wasted on needing to reinvent the wheel every morning as everyone understands the organisation's direction and purpose. Staff can relax and get on with their jobs, knowing that they're a vital cog in the organisational wheel.'

What happened to the original Quaker companies?

The answer is, most of them were swallowed up by big multi-nationals and, despite assurances, lost all of their heritage and source energy (see Chapter 6 for more about the latter). I have a friend who worked for Cadbury twice, once before and once after the acquisition by Kraft (now Mondelez). In her view, everything that was good about Cadbury was swept away. Former Sainsbury's CEO Justin King calls this the 'Kerplunk' theory, after the children's game where you have to pull out straws without all the marbles falling through. In the game, there are some straws that don't hold up any marbles and never did, and you can pull them out with impunity. Then there are other straws that you pull out and discover you've made a terrible mistake. 'I think that most incumbent executives believe that all the straws are holding up all the marbles,' Justin told me. 'And most business owners without a moral compass believe that only those straws that hold up the marbles at this moment in time have any value at all – but neither are right. There are some straws businesses hold on to that don't hold up any marbles. The reason Cadbury and Rowntree were subsumed was that they were not performing very well. I would argue that a responsible and moral business position does evolve over time and there were things they were holding on to that no longer held any marbles. For example, M&S used to perform chiropody services for their staff – and there may have been a time when that was crucial in order to be a moral employer. Cadbury built houses for their employees – at the time, that was the right thing to do. If you hold on too long, you weaken yourself commercially and that undermines the cause you want to pursue. I think a moral business needs to be sharper at pulling out the straws that are no longer relevant.'

Vittoria Varalli, in describing the turnaround at Canadian grocer Sobey's, saw that their CEO Michael Medline identified one straw that wasn't holding up any marbles: 'We changed the organisational and cost structure, but not the culture, as that was what made us great. He came in because the business wasn't doing well. What had gone wrong was that the company had been built as four regional companies, so it wasn't leveraging its scale. He nationalised the company because there was no need to have four different people buying peanut butter. We needed to graduate from being four individual fiefdoms.'

Businesses that have stood the test of time have kept strong connections to their founders and heritage (like Greggs and Sobey's), while not trying to hold on to sacred cows that are no longer relevant in today's world.

A word about B Corp

Most commercial companies are bound by their articles of association to maximise shareholder value; in the US, it's enshrined in the Constitution. The B Corp movement was set up to put forward an alternative – to develop businesses that focused on maximising stakeholder value, i.e. businesses where stakeholders are considered to be employees, customers, communities, suppliers, the environment and shareholders – the theory being that if you focus on taking care of all the stakeholders, the shareholders will be taken care of as well. The movement started in the US and, at the time of writing, has 4,088 companies certified in 153 industries across 77 countries. I was introduced to the movement by James Perry, co-chairman of premium frozen ready meals supplier COOK, one of the first UK companies to become certified. He felt that it gave them huge internal credibility. Prior to certification, many of their team felt that the company's good intentions weren't solid and wouldn't pass the test of time. After certification, the team saw that the owners were serious about their intentions and became much more engaged in this new way of being. At last year's UK Grocer Gold Awards (the Oscars of the UK food industry), they won Employer of the Year – no mean achievement for a company of their size and scale. Heart in Business Ltd is a B Corp, as are many household names. Patagonia is on the list, along with Ben and Jerry's and Alpro. Initially they were the typical B Corp. However, the movement is becoming broader and more mainstream – the North American division of dairy giant Danone is a B Corp; Weleda has just become one; Unilever has acquired a number of B Corp companies, and they are looking at it in the context of the whole corporation. If you're serious about being a heartful, purpose-led organisation, I suggest you check out B Corp in the Resources section.

Thornton's Budgens team interview #4

Name: Emmanuel Reginald
Nationality: British Tamil
Position: Operations leader
Length of service: 30 years

When we moved from a traditional style of management with everyone stuck in clearly defined areas to having an interim manager, I struggled – but things have improved greatly since the co-leadership style has been put into place. I feel free to get on with my job. I used to feel imprisoned in the hot food section, but since then I've been able to work in the Post Office. The co-leadership style is more efficient and heart centred, and people have the freedom to be more creative and innovative. It's also more cost effective, and we've been able to reduce the number of staff.

Working for Thornton's Budgens has deeply impacted my life. We raised money for Sri Lanka, I was interviewed by Jon Snow on Channel 4, and I went to several black tie events. Thornton's Budgens is not a nine-to-five job; it's a place where you are offered many opportunities to grow. I love working for a famous man who has given us all so many opportunities to experience new things. I see us as a leader in the retail world, developing great initiatives such as the plastic-free campaign.

I've used the coaching I've received at Thornton's Budgens in my personal life too. I listen more and take other opinions on board. I can give advice when asked, and be supportive and offer more independence to my children. I'm a happy and proud man to be working for Thornton's Budgens.

6

Organisational Culture

So, job done? Alas, no. Getting clear on your organisational purpose is just the starting point. No matter how brilliant your purpose statement is, it's never going to be specific enough to guide everyone on a day-to-day basis. Every organisation has a culture and it's either consciously stated or exists unconsciously. This is something I wish I'd known years ago. I think it's the single most important aspect of what defines how a company behaves in the world. When I took over my stores, they shared the Budgens culture, which was very much command and control – policing, issuing instructions, the centre knows best, and so on. It was a fear-based culture, as is common with so many retailers, where you do what the centre says, as that's where the power lies. On top of that, each store had its own unique culture. This was probably because the Budgens culture hadn't been consciously stated or consistent over time, and both stores had long-standing managers who imprinted their own interpretation of the Budgens way onto their store.

Converting an unconscious culture into a conscious one is a huge job. I've learnt how to do this the hard way, but that led to much frustration and wasted energy. I wish I'd tackled the issue of culture upfront at Thornton's Budgens, as Dave Lewis did at Tesco. Dave was clear – behaviours lead to culture, with those behaviours modelled by the leaders. Prior to his time, all the words spoken were about serving customers, but all the behaviours were about the numbers, so the culture became about the numbers. And indeed, as with the culture, the purpose of the organisation became the numbers. If there isn't a powerful, stated purpose, unconscious behaviour drives the de facto purpose. As Dave told me: 'You can't talk yourself out of something you behaved your way into. The behaviour had to be that no one tries harder for customers and that we treat people how they'd like to be treated; and that we, the leaders, behaved consistently with these values. We used behaviours to decide who stayed and who went – it wasn't just "Was he/she good at the job?", it was "Is he/she the right person for the job?" and "Does she/he have the right values?" We got rid of the offices, the executive suite, the hierarchy, the planes. "We only exist to serve customers" – when people see you do that, they know you're not just saying it. When people live one life and talk about something else, don't be surprised when the audience notices that the words and music don't add up.'

I love that last comment! How often have you heard people saying one thing and doing another? Does that inspire you to want to follow the talking or the acting? And what you can also see at work here is another part of the purpose process – what needs to go. Given Tesco's new purpose, the private jets, office suites and the old hierarchy had no role to play, so they went. When I asked Dave about supplier negotiations, he shared how the change in emphasis affected negotiating with Tesco: 'If what we were doing [with suppliers] had a good customer relevance, it could be tough but you always got there. When the objective moved from "getting things right for customers" to "getting something right for me", the behaviour [with them] went from being hard but fair, to just hard. We retrained everyone and said, "If you can't go home at the end of the day and tell your mother/wife/daughter/sister what you did today and be proud of it, don't do it."'

When I discussed culture with Aileen Richards, her take was that 'part of culture is the artefacts – such as having truly open-plan offices, the behaviour of people, the openness of people – you can go to any Mars office anywhere in the world and you'd know you were in a Mars office'. The open-plan offices at Mars helped to nurture the habit of openness, equality and having no place to hide!

The importance of source energy

A number of years ago, I did some work with author and researcher Peter Koenig, who has spent his life looking at people's relationship with money, and more recently on what he calls 'source principles', a description of what founders do to realise their projects and enterprises. His discovery was that these principles are perennial and apply across the board regardless of size or type of business. The theory goes something like this.

Every business, no matter how old, has a single founder; and when that person – or source, as he calls the founder – leaves the business and completes an orderly succession, his or her source role and values get passed onto the successor and the business can continue to thrive. If, however, the business has been sold and the 'torch' is not properly passed on, this role will remain with the founder, to the confusion and detriment of both parties. The business will struggle and may eventually fail, and the founder will find themselves preoccupied with thoughts about the business and not understand why because they thought they'd left. In an alternative scenario the founder might lose interest in the business and no longer care about its future, either in the circumstances described or even while still in office. This is tantamount to the founder 'dropping the torch', in which case someone else in the organisation, or outside it, can pick it up – maybe even unknowingly – and inject energy. This situation, however, is equivalent to a new start with a new set of values and culture, even if there are no interruptions on the surface in terms of product, service and branding.

From speaking to Justin King, it's clear to me that Lord John Sainsbury didn't approve of his successor, so didn't pass on the source energy. The business started to struggle until Justin arrived, connected back to what had made Sainsbury's great, and somehow picked up the source energy again. I'd also speculate that Dave Lewis's predecessor at Tesco didn't hold the source energy, yet Dave managed to pick it up. If a business is in flow, the CEO has the source energy – and if it's not, they probably don't. The passing on of source energy has nothing to do with legal processes or a job title – it is, as the name suggests, an energy that needs to be passed on. There's no doubt that things never fully flowed for Thornton's Budgens when we had the Crouch End store. After selling the store, and having studied this subject with Peter, I approached Martin Hyson, the Budgens director who was most likely to hold Budgens' source energy. While my business was only an offshoot of the original Budgens, I still felt it worth asking Martin if he would be willing to pass the source energy to me. He immediately got the idea and said: 'Andrew, I trust you with the Belsize Park store. I know you're the right person to lead it and that you know exactly what to do.' I really felt the impact of his words and experienced a transfer of energy. My body tingled and I felt very alive. And although I can't say there was an immediate shift at the store, things did begin to flow, and we became much more aligned to the purpose I'd created. It was almost as if, until I was the legitimate holder of the source energy, I couldn't take the business in the direction I wanted to.

I've coached a few CEOs through this process. They clearly didn't hold the source energy and their businesses were struggling. When I helped them to ask for the source energy, everything shifted. What follows is a case study, using false names.

About five years before I became involved, Peter had asked his son, Josh, to take over as MD of the family textile business that he and his wife had founded. This wasn't necessarily in Josh's life plan, but he agreed out of a sense of duty. When I explained the theory of source energy, Josh lit up – he could sense that he didn't hold the source energy of the company. He was operating in the shadow of his father and felt he was only a caretaker before passing on the business. He also felt that he needed to have the same management style as his father, even though it wasn't natural to him – in fact, he could not be authentically himself.

After some discussion, Josh agreed to take his father out for lunch. It would just be the two of them (which was not something they often did), and he'd ask him to pass on the source energy. Over that lunch, his dad really opened up to him. He told Josh that he had dysgraphia (a deficiency in the ability to write), which he'd never shared before. Even to this day Josh is unsure whether his mother or brother know. Lots of pennies began to drop into place for Josh. He now understood why, whenever there was an important letter or email to write, his dad would always ask Josh to do it for him. And that if his dad did write emails on his own, they were never more than a few words. Josh's father reached over the table and put both of his hands over Josh's, and said: 'You've achieved so much with this business that I could never have achieved – it's yours now, not mine; know that you've done what I never could have. It's up to you how you take it forward.'

As Josh shared this with me, he started to cry as he imagined himself back at that restaurant table. Josh also realised that he could let go of his dad's style of leadership, which was all about 'stop moaning and get on with it'. His dad had legitimised Josh doing things his way and was so specific in what he said that Josh really felt it. It wasn't flannel or his dad being nice to him: he meant what he said. And even though Peter had passed legal ownership to Josh and his brother years ago, for the first time Josh felt legitimate and empowered in his role as MD and could start to be authentic in how he led the company, using a more inclusive approach, addressing green issues – taking a more heartful approach. And he also felt his father had let go of a huge burden by passing on the source energy and sharing his secret with Josh. I'm pleased to report that it worked financially, as Josh and his brother more than tripled the turnover of the business.

By contrast, I found myself working with another CEO who didn't buy into the source energy idea. The original founder was still around on the periphery of the business – she didn't respect the new CEO and seemed hell-bent on destroying the organisation, even though she still saw it as her baby. The CEO thought the founder was irrelevant and had nothing to do with the issues the organisation faced. That CEO has now departed, and the new one also refuses to believe that the founder has anything to do with the mess that the business is in, even though she's clearly mobilising elements of the organisation against the CEO and the board. I believe they will continue to struggle until this matter is resolved.

Some of you may think source energy is a crazy notion and that it's all about how the CEO acts. However, if running a business is all about heart, emotions and energy rather than running the numbers, then I believe that founder energy can play a key role in its success and definitely impacts organisational culture and purpose. While it's clear to me that Dave and Justin tapped into the source energy of their respective organisations, they inherited broken businesses that needed to be fixed.

If you're still unsure about the idea of source energy, perhaps you'll find Eudora's more down-to-earth description useful: 'Founding and growing a business can feel like being a parent. You bring your baby into the world, love it, nurture it and watch it grow. One day it will be time to let go of it but, as all parents will probably agree, it's not that easy to let go. Passing on the source energy of your company takes trust and belief that it's ready to grow into something far greater than you. I recently coached a CEO who had just sold her successful business for a lot of money. She felt confused and empty. She knew she should be happy but all she could feel was a hole in her heart. It was only when she could mourn the loss of her business and wish it well that she could start looking at her empty nest and consider what the next step in her life might be.'

A word about love and fear

I believe that there are only two ways to approach life – from a place of love or fear. John Lennon once said that when we're afraid, we pull back from life and that 'when we are in love, we are open to all that life has to offer with passion, excitement and acceptance'. Living from a place of love is about being vulnerable, trusting, being grateful and being open. It's about seeing the best in people and trusting that no one sets out to do a bad job. In contrast, many organisations are run from a place of fear, with rules, consequences, sticks but not many carrots, hierarchies, command and control, and 'Do as I say, not as I do.' The word love can be threatening to some leaders, but I'm finding that there's less resistance to the L-word than, say, five years ago. As humans, we all want to be loved – so why not at work as well? Authentic Leadership is a love-based approach to managing people and an antidote to the traditional fear-based approach. Over the years, I've been accused of being too trusting and naïve. I know that I've had that trust exploited at times, at a cost to me and my business. And yet, I still argue that the positive benefits that the company and I have had from my natural trust in others have exceeded (many times over) the small cost of the times when it has been breached.

Greggs' success story

With UK baker and food-to-go retailer Greggs, the business wasn't broken, yet their CEO Roger Whiteside managed to tap beautifully into the source – the historic and clear purpose of the founders of Greggs – to reinvent the company. By doing this, he has prevented Greggs from falling into the trap that many historically purposeful businesses fall into, by failing to stay in touch with the zeitgeist. This is arguably why so many of the original Quaker companies got swallowed up by giant conglomerates and lost their sense of purpose.

Roger told me: 'We didn't find it difficult to engage with stakeholders on the purpose question, because of our long history – we relied on the history of the group to inform us. We quickly came together on the purpose, which was: "To provide freshly prepared food at great value that was accessible to everyone." Good quality, freshly prepared food is typically expensive, and we wanted to become the place to go, and for it to be easily accessible to you, regardless of where you live. Our history is all about value. Early on, Greggs' founder discovered that the people who were the most grateful for their services were the working classes – and that has never left us. Being vertically integrated, where we create our own food and don't just sell it, gives us a competitive advantage. People feel there's a purpose behind what we do; it's not just about making money, although of course we need to be successful to continue what we do. Right from the start, Ian Gregg, who expanded from his father's one shop, recognised the wider role of a business in the community in which it operated. He always had that perspective, which means he acutely saw the need to look after his employees and treat them fairly, and to be seen as a good employer. Also, being sure that the community in which they operated could benefit from what Greggs could offer – for example, his free "Pea and Pie suppers" for OAPS who couldn't afford to make ends meet. Another idea that I have reinvigorated is Greggs Outlets, which sell day-old products at massively reduced prices – both reducing food waste, which we're very committed to doing, and serving less well-off communities. We're now growing that chain in parts of the country that could not support a regular Greggs.

'My reflection on culture is that most good businesses I come across have policies about purpose, values, culture, etc. The reason why Greggs feels different is that, right from the beginning, we have walked the talk – people see we mean it by the actions we take and it's not just purposewash. The businesses that do it more consistently over time gain more trust – and that's what's happened at Greggs. We do find ourselves regularly making financially suboptimal decisions in the short term, as we feel that in the long term, they're the right decisions. We recently launched our first-ever sustainability report, called the Greggs Pledge. We spent a couple of years working on this with our stakeholders to see what we can do to be a better business. We have a great reputation, and the world is changing so much we need to keep ahead. We've picked 10 areas where we feel we can make a difference, some of which are pretty stretching, including carbon zero by 2030. The reception from our people has been tremendous. We haven't invented this; lots of others are doing it and the investment community has woken up to it. We're trying to get ahead of the game, but we can't get there in one go. Culturally we're not comfortable about shouting from the rooftops about what we do as there's a risk that people will think we're just doing this for the publicity – so the Greggs Pledge is a step away from normality for us. There's a possible cynical backlash, but customers are now expecting companies like us to do something. I'm convinced that, in the developed world, where people have a vote with their pound, they will start to vote for brands that they see trying to do this better than others. And this will only increase as the consequences of not doing this become more apparent to everyone.

'It's an exciting time. I am in my 60s, so don't expect to be in the vanguard of this, but the people in their 30s and 40s need to reinvent the entire system so that it keeps growing but does not keep destroying – and that can be done. The top can commit to it, that's not difficult. The trick is that people all the way through the organisation need to make decisions in that way too. And that's where problems arise – where people think the right thing to do is not in line with the values and purpose. If that happens too often, it impacts your reputation. The tone has to be set from the top and others will see that's how they need to behave. The longevity of Greggs really supports this – I don't think I've created any new purpose or values for Greggs; what I've done is keep the tradition going. I think it's much more difficult to change the culture. I've tried to do that – when you go in, the culture is not where you want it to be, and the people have been taught to behave in a certain way. The closer you get to the hard-nosed, short-term financial rewards type of business, the less inclined you are towards this type of conversation as everything is geared towards a sale. Then it's very difficult to shift a culture when everyone knows you're going to be flogging it soon. In any business with longevity, you can look to its legacy for proof and keep that going. The foundations for the success of the past eight years were all there – I didn't have to create anything new in terms of purpose. We weren't in a turnaround; it was all fuel in the tank waiting to be deployed with the right focus, which was on food to go rather than being a take-home baker. That wouldn't have succeeded if we hadn't had fuel in the tank about what people felt about the brand, which had been generated long before that. What we did manage to succeed in doing was overcoming the prejudice about precisely why the brand was loved by many, which the people who didn't know it well assumed to be low price, low quality. It has been a relatively recent revelation in this country that high quality can come at low prices. That's where the vegan sausage roll played a role in unlocking brand perception among Greggs' brand refusers. In the year that we sold all those vegan sausage rolls, we have never sold so many pork sausage rolls!'

There are so many aspects to this story that line up with the key messages of this book:

- ♥ tapping back into source energy through alignment with historic values and principles
- ♥ their purpose being clear and beyond profit

- consistency over time
- the need for their purpose and values to be lived from top to bottom in the organisation.

The turnaround at Sainsbury's

Sainsbury's, the number two grocer in the UK, also went off track. And while they didn't end up with the SFO being called, they were in trouble when Justin King joined in 2004. Justin realised that going back to some of the founding principles of the business was where the answers lay – in fact, this seems to be the key for well-established businesses that have lost their way.

Justin told me: 'If you read the introduction to John Sainsbury's book, he said: "I left the business in the hands of people who were unable to take forward my legacy." What he really meant was that he left a business that was incapable of being led by anyone other than him. He was the card carrier. The business didn't need to have the skill set as he made all the decisions; he was woven into it in such a way that it was not capable of being run without him. For some in business the final proof of their genius is that the business cannot survive them. When Sainsbury's was founded in 1869, it said over the door of the first shop "Quality perfect, prices lower", and today it says on the advertising "Live well for less". You don't have to try very hard to see the DNA connection 150 years later. What went wrong at Sainsbury's was that, for a period of time, because of operational dysfunction, it didn't work without its starter motor – Lord John Sainsbury – and it lost sight of all the things that made the business what it was.

'Our "making Sainsbury's great again" plan was developed before I joined, when I was on gardening leave. We wanted to reach back to everything that had made Sainsbury's great but put it in a modern context. At the core of what made Sainsbury's great was its mission, goal and values – and everything that had broken it was the execution thereof. We recreated it through a lock-in for two days at our ad agency. We pulled together a team of 12–15 people – a mixture of store staff, head office people, colleagues on tills, senior people, etc. Their brief was to go to the archive, which was at the Museum of London, dig into the past, hold listening groups – and they had about a month to do it. We wanted them to prepare a room at the agency to stimulate us. We had three rooms – ours [the operating board], their meeting room and the content room. When we went into the content room – wow! It was Sainsbury's mission, goal and values come to life in pictures, quotes, adverts from the 1920s – this incredible physical manifestation of 125 years of history. Over the following two days, we [the board] presented our ideas, and they asked us questions. We iterated through this to the point where we could send the white smoke up the chimney – with the exception of the odd word, what we produced that day stayed in place for the entire ten years of my tenure.'

Justin said that the connection with the company's culture was in 'how you communicate anything – relentless repetition, making it live in lots of real ways so that it's believable. For example, we sold the art collection, and everywhere there had been a piece of art, we put up something that told the story of the mission, goals and values – a picture of a product or shop, always annotated with a value. Every noticeboard in the company was changed – each one had a values section where we put all of the messages that related to values. With the suggestion scheme "Tell Justin", you had to identify which of the six values your suggestion related to. It got to the point where 75 per cent of employees could make a pretty good stab at the mission and values. In a business of 150,000 people, that takes some doing. The reason that it worked was not because they could chant them like a religious mantra, but that they saw the values alive and present every day.'

They went on to create a mission, goal and values course: 'The board did the course, then we finessed it into its final version. Over the course of a month, each member of the board ran a course, then each of the people who had been on the course ran a course themselves. In three months, all 11,000 leaders in the business went through that course. Every single team was then given a budget of £1,000 to run a shorter one-day course for their colleagues. One of the many things we did on the course was to do something in the community, as community was one of our six values. We put 145,000 people through a shared experience in less than three or four months – and went from no knowledge to complete knowledge in that time. The key is making it live throughout the business, where it matters. We had to relaunch the performance scheme – to move from what you were achieving to include how you were achieving it. Several years later we came up with a rewards scheme that was classic "points mean prizes". There was a catalogue and all senior leaders would have a chequebook so they could award points for something that deserved recognition. They were called LOVE (Live Our Values Everyday) points. We had to allow colleagues to keep the cheques. For many, framing the cheque and sharing it with family and friends was more valuable than the points themselves.'

To complete the story, here are the Sainsbury's mission, goal and values that Justin and his team developed:

Mission: Making Sainsbury's great again.

Goal: At Sainsbury's we will deliver an ever-improving quality shopping experience for our customers with great products at fair prices. We will exceed customer expectations for healthy, safe, fresh and tasty food, making their lives easier every day.

Values: Getting better every day. Great service drives sales. Individual responsibility – team delivery. Keep it simple. Respect for the individual. Treat every £ as if it's your own.

Justin reiterates many of the points that Dave makes about culture – you have to get buy-in, you have to be clear about what your purpose is and live and breathe it. It's all about behaviour.

Creating a safe environment

The most important precondition for a heart-centred business and for Authentic Leadership to thrive is safety. As a leader, if you want people to be themselves, then you have to create a safe environment. This will lead to a healthy culture. At Thornton's Budgens, I could've said there's no need to get permission to try out a new idea, just go ahead and do it – but if I or one of the others in the leadership team reprimanded someone for trying something new, they sure as hell wouldn't do it again. Likewise, if I encouraged people to be vulnerable and share what they were truly feeling and, when they did so, I didn't listen properly, then it was unlikely they'd feel safe enough to repeat the experience.

In 2015, Google conducted an internal study looking at the differentiators that explained why some of their teams were so much more effective than others. The number one reason was psychological safety. This is defined as 'being able to show and employ oneself without fear of negative consequences of self-image, status or career'. It can also be defined as a shared belief that the team is safe for interpersonal risk-taking – with team members feeling accepted and respected. I'm not in the least surprised by this, and if you only take one thing away from this chapter, I'd say that this is it. There's no magic formula, but much of what we write about in this book will help to create psychological safety. It takes time, it's led by example, it's precious and it can be destroyed more quickly than it can be built.

When I sold the Crouch End store, a team from Budgens managed the process. Terry, the team leader, sat in on the internal briefings when the sale was announced to my team. Everyone led by me was in tears. Afterwards Terry shared that he'd never seen anything like it and was very touched by what he saw. This is psychological safety in action. The level of trust that we built with the Crouch End team over the seven years I owned the store had created enough safety for all of us to show our true emotions. Terry also shared that, in these situations, the store teams were mostly glad to see the back of the retailer, making our situation even more unique. Again, when I announced the sale of Belsize Park, there were even more tears and emotions ran high. People felt even safer to share those emotions, knowing they would not be used against them at some point in the future.

It's worth sharing the other four factors in the Google study:

1. Dependability – team members get things done on time and meet Google's high bar for excellence.

2. Structure and clarity – team members have clear roles, plans and goals.

3. Meaning – work is personally important to team members.

4. Impact – team members think their work matters and creates change.

I hope you get a sense of the complexity of the human condition and see that, as a leader, there's plenty that you can do to help your colleagues be the best version of themselves – all of which will lead to a thriving, buoyant and successful organisation. I think Karolina's story (at the end of this chapter) is evidence that creating a safe environment really does help people to thrive.

When Eudora first arrived at the Belsize Park store, the staff were very much divided down ethnic, religious and national lines. As both the team and individuals started to receive coaching, attend Authentic Leadership workshops and be actively listened to by their managers and colleagues, the feeling of safety grew, and they were able to bring more of themselves to work. 'I remember the moment when an Eastern European manager broke down in tears in a one-to-one coaching session,' she says. 'It felt like a tipping point for the whole store. She left the coaching session and started to be more open, vulnerable and authentic in her interactions with the Thornton's team and also with customers. A few weeks later she shed a tear in public, in a team meeting. You could feel the room soften and her colleagues lean in with empathy. Her actions gave others permission to show emotion and be vulnerable. Trust, safety and connection grew exponentially.'

Here are three of the most fundamental tools I've learnt that not only helped me to open my heart, but can also be used in many different situations to create psychological safety within a team or organisation.

Tool 1: Check-in

Have you ever experienced being in a meeting and realising you'd missed the last few minutes as you'd been tied up in your thoughts? A check-in is a way of helping people to become present. It's all about grounding, which literally means getting people's energies out of their heads and into their bodies. There are many different forms this can take, and in time you'll learn to fit the check-in to the situation. Invite the group to be still, with both feet firmly on the ground, and, if they're willing, to close their eyes. Invite them to take some deep breaths with you, focusing on your breathing. Invite them to breathe as deeply into their belly as they can – and do at least six breaths together. Suggest that if they find their minds wandering, they should bring their attention back to the breath.

Ask them to notice how they're feeling. At this point, you have two choices – if it's a small group or a long meeting and you have plenty of time, you could ask them to slowly open their eyes and share how they're feeling in a sentence or two. Ask whoever feels ready to go first, and then go clockwise from there. If it's a bigger group or a shorter meeting, before people open their eyes, invite them to think about which two words best express how they are feeling in the moment. Again, ask someone to volunteer to share their two words, then go clockwise from there.

Please note that if someone shares something at a check-in, it's about allowing them to let it go and not about adding it to the agenda. However, if someone is distressed, you might need to give them a bit more space to share a little more, and ask if they'd like to pick it up with you after the meeting. A check-in is not a conversation – each person speaks in turn, and everyone else just listens without saying a word. If this all seems a bit weird, just say you'd like to do a bit of mindfulness to help everyone settle. Mindfulness has suddenly become very acceptable in the business world, whereas meditation and conscious breathing can still seem a bit 'hippy'.

I always aim to start meetings with a check-in and sometimes I do it with complete strangers. A few years ago, a colleague of mine, Sujith, and I had a meeting with the Chief Minister and CEO of Guernsey. As we waited in the government buildings, I suggested to Sujith that we take a risk and do a short meditation and check-in at the start – so I did, and the Chief Minister loved it. It got the meeting off to a great start. I believe that not only can a good check-in make a huge difference to meetings, it can also help to build psychological safety. Before we introduced self-leadership at Thornton's Budgens, we had a small group called the Team Forum, which comprised a cross-section of team members from different departments who met quarterly to discuss key issues and strategy. During a more detailed check-in, I said: 'I feel really awful today, and if I hadn't had this [important] meeting, I'd love to have stayed under the duvet for the day.' Nicole, who was next to check in, said: 'Are we really allowed to say things like that – as I feel the same?' Something shifted in the group that day, and subsequently all of our meetings were much deeper, more insightful and more productive. As the leader, I showed some vulnerability and that helped people to trust me more. With online meetings, it's even more important to do a check-in to help people connect with each other.

Finally, you can use check-ins at home. Eudora and I regularly (often a few times a day if we are together) have a check-in. It is a chance to take a moment and see how we're both feeling. We don't meditate; we just give each other space to share what's going on and listen.

> YOUR TURN: *Next time you are running a meeting at work, take a risk and use this check-in process at the start. Notice if it affects how well the meeting goes.*

Tool 2: Active listening

As humans, one of our most basic desires is to be heard. Yet, in most situations, most of us don't listen very well. Have you ever experienced being in a meeting when someone else was speaking and you were planning exactly what you were going to say next? Were you listening to what they actually said? Sadly, this often happens in the business world. Active listening is a way of doing the opposite. You can use this one-to-one or in a larger meeting. In the latter, you can create pairs. In both situations, the process is the same. The example I use here assumes it's a large group, but it can easily be adapted for a one-to-one situation.

- ♥ Invite people to pair up, take their chairs together to different parts of the room and sit opposite each other – facing each other squarely and as close to each other as is comfortable.

- ♥ Ask them to sit up straight and look each other in the eye. Help the group to decide who is going first. Before you start, you might want to do a quick grounding exercise by inviting everyone to close their eyes and take a few deep breaths before starting.

- ♥ Then invite whoever has agreed to go first (the speaker) to talk about the agreed topic for a fixed amount of time (say three minutes – use a timer to help you manage this).

- ♥ The listener looks them in the eye (even if the speaker is looking elsewhere) and just listens. As the listener, you might want to make encouraging noises, but don't say anything. The only exception is when the speaker dries up and stops speaking for an extended period (although there's nothing wrong with a little silence). In this case, you might say 'Tell me more about that', just to get them going again. No other words or comments should be uttered by the listener.

❤ When you've called time, as facilitator you could then invite everyone to close their eyes and take a few breaths. Encourage the listener to reflect on what they heard and the speaker to reflect on how it was to be heard.

❤ At this point, the listener will be invited to play back to the speaker what they heard. If the speaker was talking for three minutes, allow one minute for this. Invite the listener to do their best to use the same words as the speaker while trying to avoid paraphrasing or interpreting what they thought the speaker was trying to say. Just repeat back to them what they said.

❤ When the minute is up, ask the speaker whether the listener captured everything – and if not, ask the speaker to share what the listener missed. When this is complete, swap over and repeat.

❤ To add a bit of spice, get the listeners to introduce their partners to the bigger group, which ensures they really do listen.

At the start of this exercise, we often find people saying 'I'll never remember what the other person says!' And that's usually because most of our experience with listening doesn't involve hearing. I guarantee that if you focus entirely on listening to someone for three minutes, you'll have no problem in playing back to them what they said. I also guarantee that when you do this exercise with a group, it will shift the energy of the whole group, and everyone will feel energised by being properly heard.

You can use active listening in many situations such as team-building days or a meeting to address a major strategic issue. If you have a half-day or all-day meeting, you could start by using active listening to get pairs discussing the topic of the meeting in a way that will give everyone the chance to speak and to listen. If Eudora and I need to explore something, we'll use active listening – or she might say: 'I'd just like you to listen to me', which is her cue for me to actively listen. Try this at home and really listen to your partner – you'll be amazed at the results.

When I returned to the store after being in Germany during lockdown, a colleague popped into the 'heart room' to say hello. When I asked her how she was, she said: 'So-so.' I could've let it go but I sensed she had a lot going on. I invited her to sit and share – and she did. I just listened, and she burst into tears and shared a number of things outside work that were really affecting her. I didn't try to fix anything; I just listened and did some repeating back. I did have a suggestion about something she could do, but I held that until I was sure she had fully finished. I know she felt deeply moved that someone had taken the trouble to really listen to her. I was touched that she felt safe enough with me to cry. I know this session will have helped her process what was going on for her and it also helped to deepen our relationship.

> YOUR TURN: *Find a situation over the next few days where you can experiment with active listening. How does it feel to really listen and really be listened to?*

Tool 3: The meeting circle

If possible, it's preferable to sit in a circle for meetings rather than around a boardroom table. This is how ancient tribes met around the campfire. In a circle, the person speaking is at the 'head of the table' rather than the most senior person. There's no table to act as armour, so you're more likely to open your heart. If it's a proper circle, everyone can see everyone else, which is not always the case when you're sitting around a square or rectangular table. I encourage you to try this and even get rid of the boardroom table. I guarantee that sitting in a circle will lead to better meetings. I also recommend using a talking stick, which is from Native American culture. You place a stick (or any other object) in the centre of the circle. Whoever is holding the stick gets to talk and everyone else gets to listen – the speaker cannot be interrupted until they return the stick to the centre of the room and someone else picks it up. As with active listening, being able to speak without being interrupted allows you to develop your thinking without the fear of other people jumping in.

YOUR TURN: *The next time you're running a meeting, aim to sit in a circle – even if it means rearranging the boardroom furniture or using a different meeting room. Observe the dynamics of the meeting. Is it different from other meetings you have had with this or a similar group? If you feel it is appropriate, use a talking stick.*

Thornton's Budgens team interview #5

Name: Karolina Pauze
Nationality: Lithuanian
Position: Team member
Length of service: Five years

It's rare to find a company with such a warm atmosphere and heart-in-business values, and where the staff have such freedom. We create the company from our authentic selves. We can make our own decisions and take the initiative, but if we need help or support then it's there.

What has changed in my life since working for Thornton's Budgens and receiving coaching? Professionally, I know my opinion is valued. I know I won't be bullied. I know I'll be listened to. It's the same in my personal life. I need to take responsibility for my life because no one else will do it for me.

For example, if I want to have new products in the store, I'll ask others for their opinion, I'll listen and then decide. I love this about Thornton's Budgens – we don't need to check everything with a manager. I enjoy having this freedom. It has taught me to grow up and that it's OK to make mistakes.

I don't have much support in my personal life as my mother isn't in the UK. I've learnt that I don't need to keep ringing her, that I can make my own decisions. The coaching I received has taught me independence.

I love coming to work. I feel I've grown with the company. I feel proud because I have the best bosses in the world. I'm proud that Andrew has allowed us to grow and do what we want to do. Everyone has a voice at Thornton's Budgens. They're more involved and there's more accountability. There's no need to be scared because no one will shout at you. Instead, we're asked what happened and how the situation can be sorted out. We're one big family. It doesn't matter where you're from, you're accepted just as you are.

I trust the team, and they trust me. I have nothing bad to say about Thornton's Budgens. It's our Budgens, our company. Everyone is amazing. We laugh together, we celebrate together. I come into work even when I'm not working because I miss the team. When I'm at home, managers call to check how I'm doing. I know it means I'm important to them. No one wants to stop working for Thornton's Budgens. People stay here for many years. I see people outside work too. They're my friends, and I am very thankful.

Effective Authentic Leadership

Hopefully, it will now be crystal clear to you why Authentic Leadership is a vital skill set for these challenging times. This chapter looks at getting things done as an Authentic Leader – particularly the role of measurement and data, and my experience of structuring a heart-centred business. As leadership theorist Lance Secretan says: 'Authenticity is the alignment of head, mouth, heart and feet – thinking, saying, feeling and doing the same thing – consistently. This builds trust, and followers love leaders they can trust.'

Measuring the heartbeat of a company

There's an old adage in business that 'what gets measured gets done'. In my experience this is true, and if you want to get business leaders on board, especially CFOs (who today arguably hold disproportionate power on most boards), you have to make it measurable. My friend Anne pulled me up on this at a university reunion: 'Andrew, I totally get what you say about opening people's hearts, but you have to be able to measure it – otherwise you won't be taken seriously.' I got it, and set out on another journey. My theory was that if you could measure the heartbeat of a company through each of its employees, you'd be able to get a much better sense of how things were going than any P&L could ever tell you. The situation at Tesco is a good example of this. As the focus moved from the customer being king to the numbers being king, the reports about the culture were pretty bleak – yet each year their profits increased. Of course, as it transpired, the board and shareholders were being misled by false numbers; but with a heart index measurement in place, I believe their board would've had a much earlier warning that the train was about to crash.

I spoke with and met a number of market research companies about developing a heart index. Most said that this was already covered in their employee satisfaction measures and were not open to my view that it wasn't the same thing. One research company CEO was interested in the idea and felt that if they were going to develop a form of heart measurement, they themselves would have to open their hearts. Unfortunately, things kept getting in the way of them making a start. Meanwhile, in Zurich, my now colleague and good friend Mark Vandeneijnde and his partner Sujith Ravindran were on exactly the same path. Thanks to one of my amazing customers at Thornton's Budgens, the late Lawrence Bloom, the universe made sure Mark and I met. At one point Mark had even called his model the heart index before settling on the Human Potential Assessment. The approach is straightforward – the outputs of a business are the sum of the ways in which all of its employees show up each day (on top of the given market and environmental circumstances in which the company operates), and you can measure how these people express themselves. You can then start to see how you can grow individuals and give teams access to more of their own potential. Their approach was so aligned with what I'd been searching for that we immediately formed a partnership with their organisation, BEING at Full

Potential. We decided to use Thornton's Budgens as a case study and then Heart in Business could use the tool with our clients.

The outputs measured at Thornton's Budgens (as a small business) are mostly financial – sales, margin and costs. We used to top that up with an employee survey every 18–24 months. Mark and Sujith studied how big corporations measured input and made sure their model included the most common measures used in balanced scorecards, such as inventiveness, customer orientation and employee engagement. However, there are some important aspects that are rarely measured. Sujith examined how the Indian mystics looked at life, and many of the psychological aspects we've covered in this book are built into the below-the-waterline part of the model (Figure 2), such as gratitude, individual awareness, humility and trust vs control. The data is captured by employees filling in an 83-question survey. This is unlike most employee engagement surveys, which tend to be linear – i.e. there are a set of questions

The Framework

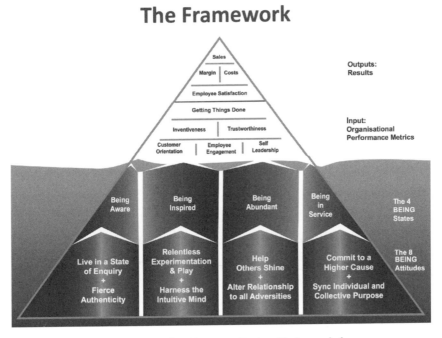

Figure 2: The Human Potential model

about your manager, a set about working conditions, and so on. With this model, the questions are used to generate 23 dimensions against which you can measure human behaviour – and how you score on each dimension is drawn from responses to a number of different questions. An individual, team or company can measure how well they're expressed on each of these 23 dimensions. I've intentionally used the word expressed – it's not that you're good or bad; what's measured is how well you can tap into that dimension.

Take one dimension: gratitude. Like all the dimensions, this has a precise definition, which is 'seeing the goodness even in challenging situations'. In this dimension, you can be not-expressed, under-expressed, over-expressed or fully expressed – suggesting that you can shift the level of your expression. When I completed my first Human Potential Assessment, I was under-expressed in gratitude. I was drawn to this as it was my lowest score. When I say I was under-expressed, I mean that I really struggled to see the good in tricky situations – like Waitrose opening in Crouch End.

It was around this time that I'd started to understand the importance of gratitude, so I worked on it. Within 18 months I had shifted to being over-expressed – by that I mean that I had shifted to having the ability to see the good in tricky situations, but sometimes taking time for this to happen. My focus on this area has continued and I am now fully expressed – meaning that I generally get to seeing the good pretty quickly, even if not immediately.

Early in 2017 the whole team at Thornton's Budgens took the survey. We wanted to understand how much potential we were using and how we could access more of it. We also wanted to see if we were accessing more of our human potential as a result of all our heart work. We didn't have anything to measure it against, so we recruited another well-run Budgens store as a control group. The store, in Islington, was in many ways similar to ours, but they hadn't done all the heart work with their people. To help us make the comparison, their team took the survey at the same time as ours. The key with this assessment is that it doesn't give you answers or try to tell you how to develop your company. I think this is great, as I always wondered, with the more traditional employee engagement studies, how someone who knows very little about my company could come in and tell me how to change things. What the Human Potential Assessment gives you is data about how people feel about key issues facing the organisation and how that's showing up to the outside world. It presents the 'now' in a unique way, allowing a trained Human Potential facilitator to work with the leaders of that company to identify how they might be able to develop their culture in a more heartful way. The examples below will give you an idea of how this works in practice.

At Thornton's Budgens, all the managers and supervisors from the store gathered together and the 16 of us sat in a circle as Mark presented the data. The pivotal chart showed how expressed we were on each of the operational performance measures (OPMs) – those drawn from balanced scorecards (Figure 3). Before he showed

Organisational Performance Metrics

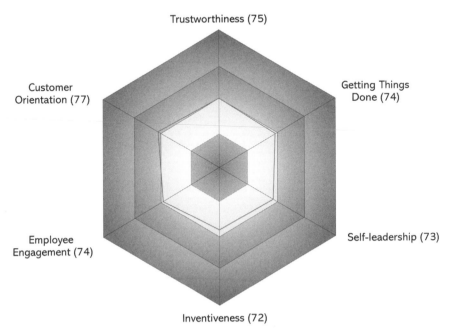

*Figure 3: Organisational performance metrics
(Thornton's Budgens)*

us the data, Mark asked the group where they felt Thornton's Budgens was the most expressed – and a few people immediately said 'customer orientation', which indeed was where we were the most expressed. Then he asked the group where they, as individuals and collectively (as a group of managers), would like to become more expressed. I agreed to stay quiet. There was silence and then, simultaneously, four or five people said 'self-leadership'. It wasn't that one said it and others copied – they said it together and the room quickly united behind this. I feel a shiver up my spine every time I tell this story as it was a pivotal moment and sent us on the journey of self-leadership – a direction the leaders of the business (and not me) had chosen collectively to help deliver our purpose. They all remember that moment and know it was their choice.

Another key moment in that meeting was a discussion about trying out new ideas and whether people needed to get permission to do so. I was very clear that they did not, and if they saw opportunities within the boundaries of our overall purpose, then they had my blessing to give it a go. I trusted them and wanted to empower them. I was told afterwards that how I expressed this came across as totally genuine and consistent with how I was as a leader, so people did take me at my word. And what was so crucial up to and after that moment was that I (and my senior colleagues) had to live up to that promise every day.

In the survey debrief, I was particularly proud that 'commit to a higher cause' was our single highest score of all the measures across the whole company. This meant that, on average, that's where we the most expressed and it showed just how well our purpose connected with everyone. And when we compared our data with the Islington store's, we scored higher on every single measure. For example, if you compare the OPMs in Figure 4 to those for Thornton's Budgens in Figure 3, you can see that our scores were consistent on all dimensions, whereas Islington's data was skewed. That suggested to me that our heart work had helped us produce a more balanced access to the total human potential of

Organisational Performance Metrics

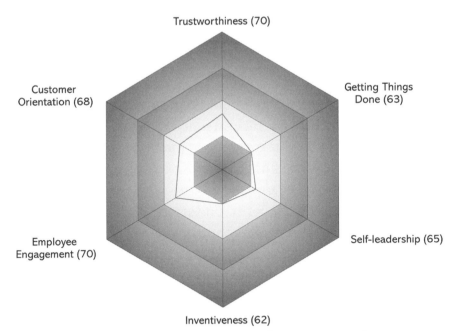

Figure 4: Organisational performance metrics (Islington)

our team. Overall, the data showed that we were using 64 per cent of our human potential versus Islington's 59 per cent. Indexed, that was 8 per cent higher; and our 2016 versus 2015 sales performance was 10 points higher than theirs – a direct correlation. Accessing 8 per cent more human potential led to a 10 per cent increase in sales. Even more astounding was that our average length of service, at 8.4 years, was more than three times higher than Islington's. Part of the trade with the owner of the control store was to have coaching sessions with Eudora and, after just three sessions, he reported that his staff turnover had significantly reduced.

Here are some other financial measures (all covering the previous 18 months):

❤ Margin: up 3 points

❤ Waste: down 4 per cent

- ❤ Packaging costs: down 31 per cent

- ❤ Repairs and maintenance: down 17 per cent

- ❤ Credit card and bank charges: down 19 per cent

In simple terms, even before self-leadership had been developed, the combination of a clear purpose and our heart approach helped our people develop a sense of care and responsibility that ensured they attended to details such as waste and packaging costs. It makes sense to me that helping people to be more authentic and harnessing more of their potential will lead to improved financial performance.

Eudora noticed a number of unexpected ways in which this process changed the leadership approach at Thornton's Budgens: 'For a lot of the team it was the first time they had been asked for their opinions. Andrew and I took the results of the survey to a Human Potential conference in India. The conference participants were so taken by the story of Thornton's Budgens that they asked if they could use the survey results as a case study. I remember a number of team members expressing their pride in the store when they knew that their voices were being heard in this way. They felt that they mattered.'

Check out the Resources section for details about how to take a (free) top-line Human Potential Assessment, which you can access via the Heart in Business website – this will not only show you how much of your overall potential you are developing; it will also detail how you score on each of the 23 dimensions.

Proof of resilience

There's no doubt in my mind that heartful businesses are more resilient, and the way we coped with the first UK Covid lockdown demonstrated that. I'd gone to Germany to recover from adrenal fatigue, so the team really were self-leading. At the time, the UK, like many other countries, was gripped with panic buying. Thanks to the agility of the team, we used multiple suppliers to keep in stock key items such as toilet paper and pasta. There were times when we stocked products that no other supermarket in our part of north London had, information that was widely shared on Twitter and Facebook. In fact, our discerning customers made the point that we didn't just have any pasta; we had stocks of De Cecco pasta, the crème de la crème of pasta!

Due to the lack of testing available at that time, anyone who had Covid symptoms (or had family members with symptoms) had to self-isolate for two weeks, meaning that, by the end of March 2020, 40 per cent of our team were off work – including both our co-leaders and five of the eight managers. Yet, despite all of this, we kept our shelves pretty full, and our sales were up 97 per cent on the previous year (Budgens' total sales in that same week were up 68 per cent). I believe that everything I've been talking about in this book allowed us to do this. How many retailers can double their sales with only half of the team and still keep the shelves full?

The impact of purposeful businesses

Our data clearly shows that the combination of heart and purpose has a positive impact on the numbers. I get that this is a sample of two stores, and while I know in my heart these numbers back up what I've experienced in person, I realise that some of you will need more convincing. The case studies on Cotswold Fayre (later in this chapter) and Musgrave (in Chapter 8) provide more hard performance data.

If you're looking for further evidence that purposeful businesses make better long-term financial returns, have a look at a paper published by Blueprint for Better Business in 2017 entitled *Purpose and Performance: The Benefits of Following the Five Principles of a Purpose Driven Business* (for a link, see the Resources section). This refers to Unilever, whose purpose is 'to make sustainable living commonplace'. There are brands within their portfolio that have a purpose (they call them sustainable living brands) and some that do not. In a study published in 2019 (available on Unilever's website), they showed that the sustainable living brands grew 69 per cent faster than their other brands and accounted for 75 per cent of their growth. In fact, they've now committed to moving all their brands to being brands with purpose and selling those that cannot make that transition. Their CEO Alan Jope stated: 'It's not about putting purpose ahead of profits, it's purpose that drives profit.'

Fortunately, more and more companies are embracing purpose and having a role in society, moving away from the Friedman doctrine of profit maximisation. Soulla Kyriacou from Blueprint for Better Business told me: 'Part of seeking to become purpose led is understanding that profit is no longer the ultimate goal; instead, it's one outcome. Of course, it's important to know that profits will still be made, even if it's not a frictionless win–win. There is evidence that such an approach works, and that it delivers long-term sustainable performance that also has positive outcomes for society.'

Vittoria Varalli told me that Sobey's always looked at the long-term game and kept their focus on their purpose ('We are a family nurturing families'). She describes it as 'our North Star, our guiding light; it underlies the way we make decisions', and that, even in tough financial times, the family stood by the business. She made another valid point: 'As we see more Gen Z people coming through organisations, it's becoming a way that people decide where they are going to work – the Gen Z generation want to work for companies with a purpose that aren't just out for profit.'

Adding heart to purpose

In *The Heart of Business*, Hubert Joly makes a compelling financial case for putting the heart back into business – using the turnaround of Best Buy and other published papers. He also quotes studies that, for example, show that the relentless focus on hitting the numbers stifles innovation. If you feel the need to explore the financial case for putting the heart back into business, I suggest you read his book. Let's leave the last word on this subject to the then CEO of Patagonia, Rose Margarito. In an interview in the *Financial Times* on 17 May 2018, she made the case for looking beyond just maximising profit, saying: 'You can serve the interests of your employees and do what's right for the planet and still make great margins.' As the company is still privately owned by the family of the founder, she says it's much easier to have non-financial bottom lines when you don't have to answer to shareholders, allowing them to have such a strong voice on environmental issues.

Case study: Cotswold Fayre

I've shared how we used the Human Potential Assessment at a company-wide level to transform Thornton's Budgens, but we've also done this with a number of other companies, one being Cotswold Fayre, the wholesale distributor of fine food and drink. We'd been commissioned to do this work for two reasons: first of all, Paul (their CEO) believed in our approach and wanted to run a more open-hearted organisation. And second, having grown rapidly from their initial seeds and gone through a very tough period a few years back, he felt they'd lost their way. Everyone at Cotswold Fayre took the survey and the results were collated. Eudora and I facilitated a discussion with the leadership team, which was split over two sessions about four weeks apart, allowing people to reflect on the data and ideas, and to subconsciously mull over what it meant. It started to emerge that part of the reason for their loss of direction was that they'd lost connection with some of the principles that Paul (the source) had founded the business on, particularly around being a disruptor, challenging the status quo and giving people the opportunity to grow through their jobs. These sessions led them to rewrite their values and actively start the process of living these new values. The management team worked on them and then engaged the broader team until the following values were settled on:

Having fun, getting it done!

We ENJOY collaborating in a dynamic environment and thrive off each other's energy and support, increasing productivity – 'having fun, getting it done'.

Building confidence through trust

With TRUST comes mutual respect. We are encouraged to take ownership, build self-confidence and be empowered to contribute ideas and have a voice in decision-making processes.

Challenging the status quo

We have the confidence to CHALLENGE the status quo and take pride in proposing and implementing new ways of working throughout our supply chain that benefit everyone involved and our planet too.

Helping others to shine

Helping others to SHINE is important. We take time and create opportunities to recognise ambition, develop individual strengths and make space for forward thinking.

Inspiring imaginations

We're open to fresh ideas, new ways and the desire to turn 'Why?' into 'What if?'. We ask questions, find answers, INSPIRE imaginations and create innovative solutions that drive change in our world for the better.

Subsequent to this, they reworked their purpose, which became: 'To benefit the people working throughout the supply chain and the people of the planet, by committing to a high standard of environmental practices.' For them, the process of engagement was just as important as it was for both Tesco and Sainsbury's. In parallel with this work on developing their purpose and values and reconnecting to the original source energy of the business, their entire leadership team took part in our Stepping into Your Authentic Leadership training programme. Since 2019, more than half of the company's staff have participated in this programme and it's now open to any employee who wishes to take part.

One of the key aspects of their purpose was to become a carbon-neutral business. As part of this, they needed to move their warehouse and logistics supplier. In Paul's words: 'This did not go well at all – in my view, without the heart work and our use of the Authentic Leadership approach, I don't think we would have survived the year without at least one of us killing one or more of the others on the management team!' When I asked Paul what the five most important learnings that he and his leadership team got out of the leadership programme and the more general heart work we did with them, he said that it:

1. Helped them consolidate the company's purpose and culture, and recreate their values.

2. Took his team away from the workplace and allowed them to show more of themselves to their colleagues.

3. Helped people to be vulnerable with each other. Seeing his vulnerability and tears made it safe for them to do the same.

4. Helped them set up company habits that reflected their culture.

5. Helped people discover other ways of knowing – using their intuition rather than their mind to make decisions.

Their corresponding financial performance was extraordinary. Sales to March 2021 were 62 per cent higher than the same period in

2019. While their 2020/21 growth was positively impacted by Covid (they supply independent retailers who generally did well during the pandemic), they are continuing to grow and are on track to add a further 40 per cent to turnover this year, which is exceptional in the mature food business.

In profit terms, the company grew by 20 per cent in 2020 and an extraordinary 162 per cent in 2021, and they're on track for a further 80 per cent growth in the year ending March 2022. I believe these numbers support the theory that being a heart-centred business can deliver great financial returns.

Using the Human Potential Assessment as a coaching tool

So far we've focused on the Human Potential Assessment at a company level, but it works just as well as an individual coaching tool. I've shared the example of my relationship with gratitude. Having worked on that, when I took the survey for the second time, I noticed that one of my lowest scores was harmony – defined as 'the ability to create sufficient space for reflection and self-care'. As is often the case, when I first saw this, I was resistant. I meditate every day, so how can I not be allowing sufficient space for reflection? My coach dug a bit deeper and helped me to identify that I'd taken the survey very much from my perspective as the CEO of Thornton's Budgens and that my working life left little space for reflection, and that maybe I wasn't as self-caring as I needed to be. So, I started to limit the number of meetings on any given day to three, maximum four. I created a weekly reflection space where I'd spend a couple of hours without any technology and with my notebook. I was delighted to realise that I could spend the morning (in Germany) on the local ski hill, scribbling notes and ideas on chairlifts or sitting in a café in the sun, and I could call that work! My diagnosis of adrenal fatigue further forced more reflection time. I have to be careful as I still tend to take on too much. I've had to change how I work. Prior to this, as the book deadline approached, I would've put in some 12- to 14-hour days of writing to get it done. I stopped doing that and still hit the deadline.

As I'm a trained Human Potential coach, I worked with the marketing director of a major food producer, whom we'll call Jack. He was curious about a score on a particular dimension that struck him as odd. When I probed into the dimension, he shared some feelings he had about the topic. When I asked him whether he'd ever had those feelings before, he remembered a childhood incident when he missed a goal in a football match and how his father had responded. He was very emotional in his recalling of the incident (which would have been 50-odd years ago), as he'd completely forgotten about it – and most likely blocked it out. In revisiting it, he realised he was still using the defence mechanisms he'd put in place at the age of six. He had a huge 'aha' moment and, with this new awareness, totally changed how he approached life. According to his CEO, he emerged transformed, and I certainly noticed a more self-assured and confident Jack from that moment onwards.

This whole journey to the heart is about unpeeling the layers of childhood-built strategies that no longer serve us – it's all part of the unknotting process Eudora has described. Sometimes, as in this instance, you get to understand why you do certain things; in other circumstances, you may not understand the why, but as long as you can see what you're doing and realise it's not helpful, you can start to change your behaviour. Awareness is always the first step towards change. Use of the Human Potential Assessment, or any other coaching tool, is merely a means to improve your awareness. Tools can help, but you need to do the work. I'm always suspicious of coaches and consultants who claim to be able to tell you what to do. Without personal insight, I don't think it's possible to make meaningful, long-term change. The Human Potential Assessment is now available on an app that allows you to continuously track your access to potential and acts as an ongoing coaching tool.

A word about structure and clarity

Structure was one of the key differentiators of successful teams in the Google study I mentioned earlier. I don't believe there's an optimum approach to organisational structure; that's very much down to the individual organisation and its circumstances. The main finding of the Google study was that teams work better when they are clear on responsibilities and structure. Their effectiveness is a function of being clear rather than the structure per se. To help illustrate this, I'll share the various structures adopted at Thornton's Budgens over the years and how they changed as we continued our heart journey.

For the first ten years, each store had a store manager, with a number of direct reports running different departments. They in turn had supervisors reporting to them. The Crouch End structure didn't change much in the seven years that I owned the store, so I'm going to focus on Belsize Park. When I bought the store in 2007, it had been managed on and off for 20 years by Jim, who was loved by the whole team – he was a great operator and knew how to be tough when necessary. His greatest skill was understanding what made his people tick and what they needed to be happy. The team's appreciation of Jim was openly shared and the stories about other managers who had run the store in Jim's absence said it all. On paper, the store's structure wasn't the easiest to understand, with quite a bit of cross-departmental working – but it was clear to everyone in the team who did what and where. At one point, I spent a month working in different departments across the two stores. In my time on the shop floor in Belsize Park, I noticed how seamlessly things worked – everyone knew what they were doing and quietly got on with it. Alas, that wasn't the case in Crouch End. I shared with Jim that to me he was like the conductor of a well-rehearsed orchestra. He didn't seem to be doing very much but the music was great, day in, day out. He was also brilliant at helping people grow and develop. Every time someone left the business or was transferred to Crouch End, another person seamlessly appeared. In the 14 years that I owned Belsize Park, every vacancy was filled internally – which was quite an achievement. The one weakness with the structure was that Jim had too many direct reports and all roads led to him. Given that he was 60 when I bought the store, that did lead to an issue with succession planning, as there was a substantial skills gap between him and the best of his direct reports. And even though Jim and I regularly discussed his plans for the future, I neglected to work on that skills gap.

When we embarked on our heart journey, I saw no need to change the structure as it worked so well. However, as we started to work on getting people in flow, we looked at improving the definition of the leadership team's roles, so we could all spend as much time as possible doing what we were good at and loved doing. For example, my role was divided into three parts:

1. The custodian of our purpose and reason for being, and the leader of our strategic direction.

2. The champion for our customers.

3. The leader of our innovation.

It was clear and focused on what I love, as well as my strengths. I felt energised by my role, and it helped me to stay in my sweet spot. I stopped doing plenty of things I hadn't particularly enjoyed doing.

The year we embarked on our self-leadership journey, Jim turned 70 and he decided he had other things he wanted to do with his life. I knew there was no one ready to take over as leader but I didn't want to recruit an external store manager. After much reflection, it was clear that I needed to recruit someone in an interim role to help the other managers grow into a position to take over the leadership. I did that without having any attachment to the structure that would emerge, as I trusted that in time it would become clear what it needed to look like. I knew a coach, Daniel, who had also managed a food retail business in north London, so he joined us as head coach with the sole aim of growing the self-leadership team so they could run the store on their own. After about six weeks, we had a crisis as the team felt that no one was in charge. Prior to that, Jim would approve all key decisions – but now there was a void. And while I didn't want one central decision-maker, the team wasn't quite ready for that level of autonomy, so Daniel also became team leader.

This transition had its ups and downs. After years of promoting people internally, having an outsider come in as team leader was never going to be easy. However, Daniel did his job of growing the confidence of the team so that they believed in themselves. The challenge was not actually about skill sets; it was all about confidence. I remember sitting with Surma (one of the senior team) after Jim had announced his retirement and discussing how she felt. She said: 'It'll be odd not having Jim to run things by.' When asked how she was going to manage this, she said: 'Well, I know what to do – it's just nice to be able to check it with someone.'

I knew when the team was ready to take over. There were four managers who stood above the rest in terms of leadership skills, and two in particular who could take over as team leader (I'd decided that the role of store manager did not fit with the idea of self-leadership). It came to me while out running one day – the either/or decision was a binary and unnecessary one. I decided to appoint Kate and Surma as co-leaders, allowing us to get the best of both of their skill sets. When I shared my plans, they were really enthusiastic and up for it. This was in marked contrast to my conversation with Surma only 18 months previously, when she was apprehensive. She had moved from being unsure about how she'd manage without Jim to being confident that, working with Kate, she could do it. They both very much wanted to involve the other two senior managers, Parvin and Marco (whose story you can read at the end of this chapter), and it was their idea that they should become their co-deputies. Over a period of about two months, the four of them worked together so that there was clarity as to who was responsible for what. And I had absolutely nothing to do with this process! While it may look like a complex structure from the outside, it worked really well and I have no doubt that what emerged was absolutely right for Thornton's Budgens.

Our various structural changes had an impact on how much human potential we were accessing on the various dimensions of the Human Potential Assessment. We amassed a huge amount of data, but here are a few highlights:

1. Having started with a higher level of access to human potential than the Islington store, by the time I sold the Belsize Park store our total overall score had further increased.

2. The areas where we recorded the greatest increases were:

   ❤ Trustworthiness: which aligns with what people said as I was leaving.

   ❤ Customer orientation: crucial in any business and a testimony to the power of helping people be more present with customers.

   ❤ Relationship to adversaries: the store team worked at previously unseen levels during the pandemic.

   ❤ Experimentation and play: self-leadership encourages both and they delivered great results for our customers.

   ❤ Harnessing the intuitive mind: giving people the freedom to go with their gut rather than having to justify everything.

   ❤ Self-leadership: hardly surprising, given our focus.

3. There was a significant dip in three of the measures during the transition period between Jim leaving and introducing co-leadership, although by the time I sold the store, all three ended up higher than they started:

❤ Trustworthiness: a new person had come in from the outside and our modus operandi went through rapid changes.

❤ Getting things done: the above did impact our ability to get things done, and witnessing this made me realise that the transition period had gone on for too long.

❤ Customer orientation: related to the above, this would have started to damage our performance had I not acted.

When Mark presented the final set of data to the self-leadership team just before I sold the store, everyone was delighted by how much the scores had shifted upwards.

Here are the lessons I learnt about structure and clarity:

❤ Involve your senior team in how best to structure things, so they have ownership in what emerges.

❤ Go with your collective intuition – really feel into what you believe is right for your organisation right now.

❤ Do everything you can to empower decision-making. Why focus decision-making around the skills of a few people when you can tap into the potential of 50, 1,000 or 10,000 people?

❤ Don't get attached to a structure – be fluid and let things evolve, going with the flow.

❤ Always keep clarity top of mind – make sure everyone

knows where the responsibility and authority lie.

❤ Change is difficult and generally people don't like it; I could've been much clearer about my expectations at times.

❤ Having a monitoring system helps to check whether things are on track or going off the rails.

❤ The transition from command and control to self-leadership is a big one and takes time to get used to – being clearer on this with the team would've helped.

Heartful leadership in action

In the interview that follows, Marco describes his personal transformation, which really was quite extraordinary. A few years back, I met Anita, a customer who had been shopping with us for 18 years, way before my time as owner. She shared this with me: 'I see the same faces and people I have for years, but they are different in how they are – they engage with me in a way they never did before and are so much more welcoming.' That is heartful leadership in action!

Thornton's Budgens team interview #6

Name: Marco Amato
Nationality: Italian British
Position: Fresh food and delicatessen manager
Length of service: 25 years

The coaching I received at Thornton's Budgens has made me a calmer person. I used to be quite abrasive and had some quite serious health issues. Now I don't worry about things anymore. I used to get very stressed, but now I take life as it comes. I've become a team player and know that together we will make things work.

Luckily, we received this coaching before the pandemic. It refocused our objectives and has helped us work around situations. The first lockdown was difficult, but we got through it a lot easier than other companies. We pulled together and got through the hard times.

I've seen members of my team change after receiving coaching. My experience is that we are a stronger team where people are more helpful and work together rather than being divisive. I'm now more open and tolerant.

The current style of co-leadership has created a good atmosphere, with people being open to change. We now feel more equal. We were able to take the best of the old and bring it forward into a new style of leadership with better communication, more equality. It was like a restart. We have disagreements but they are minor; we know we're not fundamentally different. We're all working towards the same goal and doing what's right for the store. There's a tighter bond between us.

I feel happy and fulfilled. The combination of improving my health and doing coaching and leadership training has meant that I'm in a better place now than six years ago. I'm healthier, fitter, calmer, more relaxed – and no longer angry.

 **8**

Living from the Heart

The importance of purpose (both personal and organisational) in running a heart-centred business has been a recurring theme throughout this book. However, as we continued on our journey of Authentic Leadership, I realised that, if we wanted to stand for something collectively, we needed to set boundaries and guidelines and be fairly detailed about what they were. While it's important for organisational purpose to be heavily founder influenced, what sits beneath that needs more involvement and engagement. Dave at Tesco and Justin at Sainsbury's had more experience than I did, and they prioritised sorting out their organisational values in the first 12 months.

At Thornton's Budgens, we set out to develop these together. One key part of the process was that I wanted to involve all full-time team members (about 40 people) and the key part-timers in some way. We asked Mark and his colleague Vanessa to facilitate the process, as it was crucial for me to be a participant rather than a leader. A cross section of about ten of the Thornton's Budgens team joined us and we set out to create what would later be called our manifesto. Words such as 'letting go', 'trust', 'daring' and 'authentic' started to flow. It was clear early on that the word 'values' didn't sit comfortably with the team and someone suggested 'mindsets', which quickly led to 'heartsets' – and this immediately stuck.

Over a period of two months and with numerous small group sessions, our manifesto emerged. In one session about ten people helped to write the heartsets. The style of writing some as 'I' and some as 'We' emerged, and there was a debate on each one and whether it should be an 'I heartset' or a 'We heartset'. One person had a strong issue with a proposed heartset – so it was worked on and developed until everyone felt comfortable about it. Opposite is the final version of the manifesto.

The purpose, the why and the how are self-explanatory, and it felt important to mention self-leadership before detailing the heartsets. We then needed to consider the habits we would practise to help us deliver the heartsets. As I mentioned in Chapter 4, whether it's personal or organisational, with all changes in behaviour, you need practical means to anchor them. We'd already been practising a lot of what's in the manifesto, but this was a way of capturing and formalising it. Other parts were developments and clarifications – nothing was brand new. At the drafting stage, I showed it to Booker CEO Charles Wilson. As always, he put on his customer hat and asked what was in it for him – leading us to develop the final section.

Did we fully live this every day? No! Did we refer to this when we were stuck on a particular issue? Always! Could we have lived this more? Yes! How will this manifesto fare under new ownership? Only time will tell. I recently showed the manifesto to a very experienced Irish property entrepreneur who had made his millions, lost them and made them again. His comment was: 'If every company was run this way, the world would be a far better place.'

OUR MANIFESTO

THORNTON'S Budgens

Our Purpose

We are the Community Supermarket that really cares about People & the Planet.

Why

We believe that business has a responsibility to be a force for good in society, that's why we look after our employees, our customers, our community, our suppliers and the environment.

How

Through Self-Leadership, 'heartsets' and every team member having a share in the profits.

Heartsets

Listen and learn | I believe in myself | I am mindful
We acknowledge and appreciate | We can do it
We are all respected | We bring these heartsets to life through habits

Habits

1. Active listening
2. Receiving and giving coaching
3. Giving appreciation daily
4. Living Self-Leadership
5. Being In-flow and having fun
6. Clearing disagreements 'healthily'
7. Being on the pitch and not in the stands
8. Asking for support
9. Pausing and reflecting (including check-ins)
10. Sitting in circles
11. Owning our numbers and acting on them
12. Holding ourselves and others accountable

Our Commitment to our Customers

1. We care for our community here in Belsize Park
2. We acknowledge and appreciate our customers
3. We continue to innovate so that we deliver products/services that our customers want
4. We take on campaigns that will make a difference on issues that matter
5. We do so with a smile!

Communication to customers

The final piece of the jigsaw was to capture the essence of the manifesto for customers. I believed they would pick this up through the way we behaved and interacted with them, but the classically trained marketer within me didn't want to leave this to chance and needed to communicate it in a structured way. We engaged the ZoneBrand agency in Dublin, who distilled our manifesto into some simple messaging. We also published the full manifesto in the store and on the website so that customers could read it in full if they so wished. I have no idea how much of a difference each of these stages made, but as a package, I believe it helped us to be clearer and stronger as a team and gave us a better chance of delivering on our purpose, feeling fulfilled and making a difference in the world. And while this may seem a long, drawn-out process, for me it was worthwhile. The fact that every key person in the business had some involvement meant that everyone connected to the manifesto. As we saw with Tesco, the most important aspect of all is that the leaders of the business live and breathe the purpose and values through their everyday behaviour. That gives the opportunity for others to follow. The fact that Mars's Five Principles were developed long before I worked there didn't matter; what made the difference was that I felt that everyone in the business lived by them, so who was I not to?

Case study: Musgrave

Musgrave, the former owner of Budgens, went on their own heart journey after selling Budgens to Booker. In fact, the sale of the UK business provoked the internal self-examination needed to make that shift. They are a family-controlled business and the market leader in Ireland, with brands such as SuperValu and Centra, which are all independently run (as franchises), as they believe that food retail is such an important part of local communities. Chris Martin was their CEO from 2005 to 2020, having joined 18 months previously as CFO. Prior to that he worked for PepsiCo, Asda and Storehouse and was CEO of Mothercare.

There are so many parallels here to the approach described in this book. Chris also grappled with issues such as measurement, impact on him as a person and impact on the performance of the business. 'Purpose played a huge role in redirecting the business,' he told me. 'You have to understand Musgrave's heritage. It's a family business that was founded in Cork in 1876. Its purpose only really came to the fore after the sale of the British business – which represented 40 per cent of the group. Everyone believed they were working for this international retailer/wholesaler and that was the mission going forward. There were lots of challenges in the British market and some own goals. A lot of people became demotivated about where the business was going and, when we sold it, there was a hole. What I've learnt as a leader is that you have to nurture your brand and set a direction for your business. We'd done a lot of work to be clear about how each of our brands would win in their segments. Take SuperValu – "Real Food, Real People", independent stores run by people in their community. That worked, but not well enough as it didn't have the right culture behind it.

'In the work we've been doing since 2013, we recognised that we had to give people more of a say in the purpose of the business. We had good brands but had to grow alongside the discounters, who were growing exponentially. We had to get our teams together to give them tools to grow the business, so we brought in a company, Breakthrough, to help us with this. It was about stripping the business back. The big "aha" moment was that it was nothing to do with growing the business; it was to do with growing people – giving them the time, space and tools for them to grow how they wanted to. Out of that came the fact that people were coalescing around the real purpose of Musgrave. It sounds basic, but what Musgrave does really well is supporting independent retailers in their own communities who have to be in business for the long term and need to grow to be able to invest in the future. The language started to change: "I get I have to personally grow but I'd like to see the business also have a really clear purpose and direction." That's where "Growing Good Business" came from. Our engagement scores were really good, but once we majored on purpose together with developing the right culture, the engagement scores increased exponentially. We could see that in terms of people going that extra mile and bringing new ideas. A great example is Frank and Honest Coffee. In Ireland coffee is fairly underdeveloped, but we do have Starbucks and Insomnia. In the space of four years, the team that said they wanted to work on coffee had developed the biggest brand of coffee in Ireland. The innovation around that stemmed from the work we did on purpose, as that's how we can deliver Growing Good Business. When I left, it was turning over €80m per annum.

'People want to come to work to be successful and be part of something they give their all to; so, a purpose that's seen to be true and lived by the organisation is fundamental to the culture of the business. Having come out of Britain, the challenge was how to grow, and asking what growth meant to people in the organisation. What I learnt with Breakthrough was that people need to be given tools that allow them to grow and move themselves forward. Breakthrough was very simple – around your thought processes, how you turned up, about magical thinking, about how to be part of the team, not be a prisoner, how to improve what you do. Ultimately personal growth is about the ladder of mastery – you do the same things over and over, and you get better and better. Connecting personal growth with business growth was key; it was perhaps a product of millennial thinking about how to improve yourself, your health and so on. People had honest discussions – we had some who decided the business wasn't for them. It was about relating purpose to a personal journey, not just bettering yourself but also bettering the organisation. The classic question Breakthrough asked was: "Why are you here?" It took people out of their comfort zone and their cynical views – they realised they had a short life and needed to ask what they were going to do with it. It included everyone; the leadership had to be part of it – that was critical.'

The Breakthrough process Chris describes is similar in many ways to the approach we've put forward in this book. And I love the key insight – it wasn't about how they could get the business to grow, it was about how they could support individuals to grow. Just like at Thornton's Budgens, when that happens and there's a clear purpose, the business will thrive.

Chris went on to describe some of his own personal journey: 'With this process, I realised there were things I was doing to myself that weren't positive – I had allowed myself to get stuck in the here and now. The great thing about the last few years at Musgrave was getting clearer on the outcome we wanted to achieve. Purpose needs to have the right culture and the right outcome. One of the magical things was saying to the business: "Where do we want to be in 2025?" People struggled to put themselves in the future. If I'd been less stuck in the here and now, but thinking about how to break out of that, I'd probably have suggested selling the British business two or three years earlier because it wasn't doing the retailers any good, and it wasn't doing Musgrave any good.'

Chris's use of the words 'stuck in the here and now' was about him not being present and not being in flow. He went on to share how he had changed: 'What Breakthrough encouraged was better listening rather than just hearing – being part of the conversation rather than just taking it in. We had everyone sit in a circle and reveal themselves. As CEO, I had to share what some of my challenges were. Having that honest conversation and being prepared to open up and admit there were areas I wasn't good at and needed support in was a way of bringing people on side. As a leader, I would've been tough in my demands, but I became more forgiving – not just letting people make mistakes but learning what we could've done better, and building trust by putting myself in the middle of the team. I shared who I am, what I want, what drives me, my family – being real. My human side came out in the last five to eight years at Musgrave. My wife would say I'm a better listener and far more aware of what makes people tick. I'm still very driven and outcome focused, but now I bring people with me on the journey. For her the other big change has been me being clearer on the outcome for us as a family.'

When I asked Chris about measurement, he said: 'Measuring the changes is critical, and that's where you are way ahead of what we did. We moved away from a very long-winded census every two years to something that was rapid fire with commentary that could be acted upon.' And the results? 'We had sales and profit growth every year, even with the discounters. The local commentary was that Musgrave would be the loser – the domestic company competing against the international challengers, Tesco, Lidl and Aldi. Yet, at the end of 2020, SuperValu, Centra and Marketplace were all market leaders in their segments. In fact, Musgrave as a whole grew by 14 per cent – even though they are a substantial supplier to the hospitality sector, which was closed for large parts of 2020. And, during the process I have described, in the space of one year there was a 10 per cent improvement in employee engagement across 10,500 colleagues.'

Despite world-class competition, SuperValu is now the Irish brand-leading supermarket. In fact, I don't know any other market in the world where an independently operated brand is the market leader.

Here's my summary of the Musgrave story:

- ♥ They became clear on their purpose: Growing Good Business.
- ♥ They helped their people connect their individual purposes with that of the business.
- ♥ They created a new culture that lined everything up behind their new purpose.

- ❤ They found new ways to live their values.
- ❤ The leadership team modelled those behaviours.
- ❤ They used habits to anchor their values.
- ❤ The leadership team increased their self-awareness, which gave them choices.
- ❤ By committing to open sharing and vulnerability, they created psychological safety.
- ❤ This allowed people to be more authentically themselves.
- ❤ They created a culture that achieved extraordinary business results.

I can see that they closely tracked everything we have recommended in this book and the results are as I would have expected.

Innovating with Heart and Purpose

This final chapter aims to tie everything together by showing what you can achieve when you put the heart back into your business. First, I'd like to introduce the concept of 'sphere of influence'. The theory is that if you concentrate your efforts on the things you can change, your sphere of influence grows. Even before I was introduced to this idea, I intuitively used it at Thornton's Budgens. In the very early days, I identified the environmental challenges associated with the food business and saw that a tangible action we could take to make a difference to our customers was to change the perspective around carrier bags (see Chapter 1). It was noticed, and our sphere of influence in the food retail industry grew.

In 2008/9, some people in the environmental movement wanted to draw manufacturers' attention to excess food packaging by encouraging retailers to allow customers to leave unwanted packaging at stores, and for the retailer to send it back to the supplier. We were approached by numerous people, including customers, to do this. I knew it would have zero impact on the likes of Unilever or Mars if a two-store operator like Thornton's Budgens sent them some packaging that our customers felt was excessive, but if Tesco or Sainsbury's did it, then they would listen and act. Instead, we put the energy into initiatives such as Food from the Sky and chiller doors (see Chapter 1), each of which increased our sphere of influence – with the former doing that on the international stage. Roll forward a few months to The Grocer 100 Power List, in which I featured at number 100. An independent retailer had never appeared on the list before (or since, as far as I know). Each time we made a significant move within our sphere of influence, that sphere grew. Contrast that with the earlier days at Thornton's Budgens, when we didn't have a clear purpose or know how to run a business with an open heart. And while we were successful with a number of ideas, the ones that got me on the Grocer Power List, we did waste a lot of energy on projects that were never properly completed or had a chance to take off because my focus had moved on to the next thing or the team never really engaged with them.

I want to focus on the two major innovations that we created with our open heart and purpose, which I believe have had ripple effects way beyond one shop in north London. The first is heart itself. It's a virtuous circle – without open hearts, we couldn't have developed our ways of being. And without those ways of being, we couldn't have further opened our hearts to achieve what we have, and this book may never have been written. The second is our plastic-free campaign, which I believe is the most impactful thing we ever did at Thornton's Budgens. We made this impact for a number of reasons:

- ❤ We gradually increased our sphere of influence through actions that would make a difference – so that, when we launched our plastic-free campaign, it was taken seriously by the food industry.

- ❤ We had a purpose that clearly stated that we really cared about people and the planet.

❤ Our heart work meant that people were fully committed to our purpose and could see that we could make a difference.

❤ Our timing was perfect – as Chris Martin shared with me: 'You took leadership when no one else in the industry was.'

While I don't want to overstate our role, based on the feedback I received from industry CEOs and the flurry of activity from grocers around the world after our initiative, I firmly believe that we managed to achieve a worldwide shift in the relationship between supermarkets and plastic. If nothing else, I believe we have made the case that if you want to make a difference in the world of business, opening your heart is a good place to start.

Launching our plastic-free initiative

In the spring of 2018, the Dutch chain Ekoplaza announced the world's first plastic-free aisle, and quite rightly gained a lot of coverage for this great initiative. This came hot on the heels of David Attenborough's *Blue Planet 2* series, which beamed the plastic crisis into people's living rooms. Suddenly, the crisis that campaigners had been trying to highlight for years went mainstream. I'll admit my first response to the Ekoplaza announcement was: 'Damn, we should've thought of that!' As I was pondering this, I attended a Conscious Business Lab event and met Sara Vaughan, one of the team from A Plastic Planet (APP), the social enterprise behind the plastic-free aisle. Sara said I needed to meet their co-founder, Sian Sutherland. That July, Sian came to the store and, together with a few of the team, we watched the film *A Plastic Ocean* (if you haven't seen it, it's on Netflix). The part that struck me the most was the scene where they sent a remote unmanned submarine into the deepest, least-explored part of the ocean. The seabed was lined with single-use plastic drink bottles – chucked there by us humans. Sian shared their mission – 'To help people turn off the plastic tap' – and the fact that most humans are now plastic addicts, without any awareness of how to go into recovery. For me and my colleagues, it was clear we had to do something because we could – it was our duty, part of our *swadharma* (see Chapter 1). With hindsight, I can see that everything we had done together at Thornton's Budgens had been in preparation for this moment. It was also clear to me that we could not do this alone and would need support from APP, including a full-time person from their team based at the store. I knew that running the store was a full-time job and we had no spare resources – but that, partnered with an expert, we could make huge strides. Thanks to our sphere of influence, Sian took us seriously.

At the end of August, we gave the project the green light. We agreed that we'd launch the first (and second in the world) plastic-free aisle in the UK. We also agreed to develop the idea and introduce plastic-free zones across each of our categories rather than one single plastic-free aisle, as shoppers would find this easier to use than having all the plastic-free products together. Our goal was to launch 1,500 plastic-free products by 5 November – that was ten weeks away! Even with self-leadership, there are times when it's appropriate for the owner to set the bar high – but the key people at Thornton's Budgens were all on board too. Why 1,500? Well, Ekoplaza had launched with 750 and, with all their learnings and the progress APP had made in the months since their launch, why not go for double? And why 5 November? I felt that Guy Fawkes' Day in the UK seemed a fitting launch day. Our plan had three objectives.

1. To reduce the amount of plastic that we at Thornton's Budgens were responsible for releasing into the environment.

2. To give the customers who wanted it the chance to reduce the amount of plastic that they consumed.

3. To show our larger competitors that reducing plastic usage in a supermarket was a lot easier than they were claiming.

We had three strategies to achieve these objectives, which I'll explore in some depth.

Strategy 1: Look at where we could remove or replace plastic packaging from products we packed or directly sourced ourselves

We realised we could easily make an impact with fruit and veg. About 60 per cent of our products were pre-packed in plastic, with 40 per cent being loose. Over the ten weeks, we gradually increased the loose produce until we had an 85:15 mix. We re-merchandised so that all the loose produce came first, and we had a small section at the end of the run for the products that needed to be kept in plastic, such as berries, salad leaves etc. Then we tackled other areas, some of which were easy enough, some of which took a fair bit of trial and error. Like most fishmongers, we wrapped our fish in flimsy paper and then put it in a plastic bag. With some experimentation, we found that if we wrapped the fish in a stronger wax-proof paper, we could seal it with the (paper) price label and wouldn't need a plastic bag. Bread was a tricky one. We set off to replace the aerated plastic sleeves that most retailers use with paper. Our first attempt covered the entire loaf – and sales dropped, as customers couldn't see what they were buying. The next attempt had too little paper, leaving the product too exposed – again, customers were not happy. The final version was a half-paper-wrapped product. We also had more than 200 different types of cheese. Many were sourced in blocks and cut and wrapped in the store in clingfilm – a cheap and easy-to-use material that allows the customer to see the product. Our initial trial was in a heavy waxed paper – but sales dropped as customers couldn't really see what they were buying, and it took us four times longer to wrap the cheese than in clingfilm. In the end APP found a small compostable cellulose bag that we could use. We sourced compostable containers for products such as salads, fish and meat that we cut in store and pre-packed for customers. These worked well for salads and fish but bombed for meat. And they also left us with a challenge – the packaging needed to be industrially composted, but our local council did not have these facilities.

We also had to work with our concessions. At the time we had three independent businesses that operated from our store – a florist, a juice bar and a sushi bar. Finding flower solutions was easy. The owner of the juice bar was very attached to the exact type of cup they used and was not easily persuaded to move to a compostable option. It was his business, so while we could do everything in our power to persuade him to change, we could not force him. In fact, it took a change in operator and two years to get there. With sushi, our concession used seven different types and sizes of packaging – and only two were available plastic free. During 2019, thanks to some great work with a packaging supplier that APP worked with, we almost had solutions for all seven. Our sushi partner seemed ready to roll this out, but then the pandemic hit, so unfortunately the sushi is still served in plastic.

Strategy 2: Source externally manufactured products that were plastic free, replacing plastic-wrapped products

While the major branded manufacturers were slow to see what was going on, many smaller innovative producers and start-ups recognised the opportunity. APP has a plastic-free mark that suppliers can apply for, and we pretty much guaranteed to give any product with the mark a try. These products replaced existing equivalent ones. In the case of products that were de-listed, I wrote to the supplier CEO telling them we had removed their product and replaced it with a plastic-free one – saying that we'd have them back if they produced a plastic-free version. I'm realistic enough to know that the major branded suppliers did not initially fall within our sphere of influence. Yet, as the major retailers started to take some serious steps, the branded suppliers took notice and started to visit us, expanding our sphere of influence. When it came to local suppliers, we did have an influence. Diana's Chocolates put all their effort into developing a plastic-free solution, so they were back on our shelves quite quickly. My personal favourite product was the best bacon I've ever tasted, from happy and loved pigs, packed in a (home) compostable wrap inside a cardboard sleeve. Alas, it was pricey, so we couldn't justify keeping it on the shelves. Most of these new products thrived and remained on the shelves; and those, like the bacon, were easy experiments that we could try and then move on from. Sure, we may have had a small amount of waste/stock write-offs, but in the overall scheme of our costs, they were insignificant.

Strategy 3: Bring together all of our plastic-free products into zones so that customers could easily find them, clearly marking these areas as plastic-free zones

As we headed towards the end of October, we needed to plan a full store re-merchandising that brought all of our new products, alongside our existing plastic-free ones (such as tinned products and glass bottles), into 28 plastic-free zones. There were times when some of the joint APP/TB team wanted to delay until January, but I took the view that launch day was only a line in the sand and whether or not we reached 1,500 lines by early November didn't matter – the idea was to start the journey. As part of our launch strategy, we'd worked with the branding agency APP had worked with on Ekoplaza, and I also visited one of their stores in Eindhoven, making sure we were not starting from scratch. We used APP's PR agency to ensure what we were doing got the maximum exposure and that both customers/potential customers and other retailers knew what we were up to. As 5 November fell on a Monday that year (a bad day for press, apparently), we moved the launch to

Thursday 8 November. The customers I spoke to in the run-up, and thereafter, were all positive about what we were doing.

In launch week, I took part in a number of local junior school assemblies. Each time I asked the kids if they'd seen *Blue Planet 2* – and most hands went up. They knew exactly what the issue was, as well as the solution (reducing single-use plastic), so I hoped they'd go home and encourage their parents to change. The few days before launch were pretty hectic and yet, due to the amazing work of the joint team, everything came together on the morning of 8 November. I don't want to underestimate just how much hard work this was. I often say that I take all the glory – doing press interviews, talking at conferences and writing this book – yet it was the TB/APP team that burnt the midnight oil, night after night, to get us to launch day. We'd managed to reach 1,800 plastic-free products, 20 per cent more than our very ambitious target. We had an official cutting of the ribbon by two actors and loyal customers, Jim Broadbent and Dame Janet Suzman. They were both hugely supportive of what we'd achieved, and I really felt their care when they spoke on the day.

The customer response was amazing. Our total sales in the first week after launch were 6 per cent up on the previous year and, after two weeks, that settled down to a 4 per cent increase, which was sustained for a full year – that means 4 per cent in TOTAL store sales. If you've ever worked in grocery retail, you'll know that's a big number. You can spend millions on a store refit and not get anything like that kind of response. The feedback we received was like nothing else I've experienced in my 15 years as a retailer. Our customers all got it and rewarded us by shopping with us more often – they said they wanted to spend their money with businesses that were committed to a better future and were doing something about it. They were sceptical about the leading UK grocers – saying that all their claims were too vague and too far into the future.

I recently visited a branch of one of the main UK supermarkets. There were huge posters everywhere saying they were committed to reducing food waste and that 87 per cent of their stores now gave their food waste to local charities, but there was no indication if this branch was one of the 87 per cent and to whom the waste was going. There were also big claims about reducing plastic, yet nothing in the store to indicate what they had done and in which categories. This approach leads customers to suspect greenwash. Customers saw us walking the talk and they loved it. We also attracted new customers who'd heard about what we were doing and came to see for themselves. One woman from south London emailed to thank me, saying that she now travelled an hour on a bus each way once a week to shop with us, as no one else offered a plastic-free range like ours.

Part of our success in attracting new customers was the extraordinary PR campaign run by APP's agency Higginson. I'd expected good PR and coverage but was blown away by how much we actually got. We were in all the major national newspapers; I went live on Sky News and the other TV channels covered us too. And the coverage was global, including an appearance on a CBC documentary in Canada, which subsequently led to a visit from Sobey's, the leading Canadian food retailer, and an invitation for me to visit Canada to speak at a few events and share learnings with them. In the words of Vittoria Varalli: 'Customers wanted us to take plastic out, and we wanted to take care of future generations by taking out plastic and ensuring they have a vibrant planet in the future. Our purpose is "A family nurturing families" and sustainability is an extension of this – the families of today and the families of the future.'

Over the course of the next three to six months, every major food retailer in the UK and many from further afield came to visit, along with many of the major manufacturers. We openly encouraged visits and made all our learnings and material available on an open-source basis – we actively wanted others to copy us. I know from the discussions I had with those retailers and their actions over the following 12 months that our initiative did influence huge change worldwide. I also received a message from an old contact who'd been at Iceland in the UK – he was now working for a major retailer in the Middle East and implementing plastic-free reforms there. We also won a stack of awards, including Most Sustainable Retailer of the Year at the Retail Industry Awards, the NACS European Convenience Retail Sustainability Award and, most importantly, The Grocer Gold Green Initiative of the Year. This is our industry's Oscars, with a black tie dinner at London's Guildhall. At that event, I was approached by Tesco CEO Dave Lewis, who was impressed with what we'd achieved. After a number of meetings and visits to their plastic-free trial store, Dave invited us to act as a pilot store for packaging reduction trials for the Tesco organisation. This was on the basis that we were a speedboat while they were an oil tanker – they saw the speed at which we managed to act and wanted to benefit from this. When I interviewed Dave for this book, I asked him what drew a global chain with 5,000 stores to want to work so closely with a single-store independent. He said: 'Two things – there was an emotional reason and a rational one. The emotional reason was that you clearly cared. You were trying to do something from a relatively small base – and that showed dedication, commitment and purpose. The rational reason was that Tesco is very good at taking simple ideas and scaling them – but it's really bad at being agile and flexible.' He finished by saying: 'Your life would have been easier without it, maybe even more profitable without it, but you were committed to it – and I've always been drawn to people who have a personal passion for things that matter.'

A launch to their supplier base was planned for April 2020, but then Covid came along, and the plan was swept away, along with so many other things. Looking back on our three objectives:

1. By early 2020, with 2,600 (out of approximately 13,000) plastic-free lines, we significantly reduced the amount of plastic used in the store.

2. Our customers (old and new) have managed to reduce the amount of plastic they buy.

3. Major retailers saw what we managed to do in ten weeks, and realised they could and should do more.

Another key measurement we hadn't really considered before was food waste. Many of the major retailers had cited risks of increased food waste as a reason not to reduce plastic, with the extended shelf life of a plastic-wrapped cucumber being held up as an example. When we looked at food waste eight weeks after launch, we found that we had no increase in food waste at all – in fact it had slightly reduced. And while other retailers had experienced big increases in produce waste when they moved away from pre-packed to loose, we did not. Part of the reason for this was how we approached our merchandising and the fact that we changed our equipment so we could achieve great visual impact with a fairly low quantity of stock. Our use of alternative materials didn't push up the price either. In many areas such as produce, bread and fish, our new approach did not add to costs. Where we needed to use compostable packaging, costs were higher – but with a total sales increase of 4 per cent, we could easily afford to absorb them. And in the three years since launch, there has been a lot of innovation, especially with paper-based packaging. Cost does not need to be an excuse for inaction. We didn't have time before the launch to look at zero packaging (where customers bring their own containers to refill with bulk products), so we launched a zero-packaging area the following year.

Covid hugely impacted consumption of single-use plastic. Outside of its obvious use for masks and other PPE, food such as bread had to be fully wrapped in plastic again. The amount of pre-packed fruit and veg has also increased, but only slightly. And while single-use plastic consumption has spiked upwards, I know that consumer awareness of both the climate and plastic crises has dramatically increased. In the long term, we'll see an even greater awareness of the need to reduce single-use plastic and the demand from consumers for solutions from retailers and suppliers will continue to grow – leading to many more opportunities for innovating with heart and purpose.

The 10 components of a heart-centred business

We've outlined the ways in which you can run a heart-centred business, given you tools and techniques to help you implement them, and demonstrated why this approach makes sense. Here's a summary of what it takes to be a heart-centred leader in a heart-centred business:

1. **Clear purpose:** It all starts with the business having a clear purpose – a purpose related to being a force for good in society.

2. **Personal purpose:** It's vital that the leaders (and people as deep into the organisation as possible) have a clear view of their personal purpose and that their purpose is aligned to that of the organisation.

3. **Psychological safety:** You need to create a safe environment to achieve any of this.

4. **Authenticity:** This will enable people to be authentically themselves.

5. **Culture:** With this in place, you can start to create the culture needed to deliver your purpose, which everything you do as an organisation must line up behind.

6. **Ways of being:** You can then define the ways of being that will deliver your purpose. For a company, it's a collective process. A set of values is the most common method used by companies to describe how they want to operate.

7. **Modelling behaviour:** The leaders will need to model these ways of being through their behaviour, which needs to be authentic.

8. **Habits:** You need to anchor the ways of being with habits.

9. **Self-awareness:** To create a truly open-hearted culture, you need a self-aware leadership team who can choose how to act effectively.

10. **Win–win:** All of the above will allow you to deliver a win–win, I'm OK, you're OK culture.

As Eudora says: 'Andrew and I developed these principles not through sitting at a desk and thinking what would sound good but through trial and error, experience, getting things wrong and learning from our mistakes. We continue to grow and learn each day, trying to remain humble with humour as we navigate our Heart in Business journey together.'

This whole process is a continuous learning one. I get an insight, I learn; I make mistakes, I learn; I fall down, I learn. It creates an environment where I as a leader and we as a company keep learning and growing. And you need to measure what you do and track that on an ongoing basis. In Chapter 4, Shanthy shared how our colleague Seelan had concluded that the heart experiment had failed when I announced the sale of the store. He challenged me at the final Human Potential Assessment debrief – and it was certainly a thought-provoking question, one I've pondered a lot since then. On reflection, it's hardly surprising that I disagree with his conclusion. I believe that the experiment has been a success – and here are some of the reasons why.

As Shanthy pointed out, the fact that Seelan was prepared to stand up and challenge me, the elder white man, in public, is evidence of the fact that opening our hearts has worked. It meant that he and his colleagues were fully engaged to the extent that they felt safe to challenge their leaders. Building on this, the team of leaders at the store have grown in confidence, so much so that they could manage the Covid crisis without me and do an amazing job. Every single person at Thornton's Budgens has grown as an individual and many reported to me that this had a huge impact – not only at work but also with their families and in their communities. Plus:

- ❤ We made a huge difference in the world of food retailing, especially with our plastic-free campaign.

- ❤ We developed the heart-centred way of being and are making a difference in how businesses are run. It's an approach that I believe will come of age. The self-leadership skills of the team gave me the time to work with Eudora to develop this heart approach.

- ❤ Of approximately 20 branches of Budgens that were originally franchised in London, only ours and one other survived. And we were the sole single site survivor.

- ❤ In financial terms, as the only shareholder I made a good living from the business for 15 years and put a decent amount of money in the bank at the end of it – my pension!

After my departure from the store, I had a few important conversations with former colleagues. One expressed her deep gratitude at the chances I had given her to grow and become an Authentic Leader. The trust I had in her and the coaching/training she received helped her rise to the challenge. She's had a really tough time outside work recently and shared that all of this 'helped me cope with what was being thrown at me by life. I can now stand up for myself, am aware that my inner voices are just that – voices – and I know how to take care of myself.'

The second colleague reminded me that in the early days of our coaching, we used the StrengthsFinder questionnaire (see Resources) to help people understand themselves better. Having embarked on a master's degree since leaving Thornton's Budgens, she had to complete a similar test. In comparing the results (with her original questionnaire around seven years ago), she noticed how much more caring and people orientated she is now. This shows that heart work is indeed transformative!

Eudora has also witnessed the transformation at Thornton's Budgens: 'When I first arrived, I saw a group of people who behaved like cats, all doing what they felt was right, in their own way. Now I see a team, a herd of buffalo, working together and moving in the same direction – communicating, sharing, caring, bonding. I see that the local community feels supported and safe. I see new customers noticing that there's a different energy in this store and wondering what it is that makes it feel different. Then they return because this energy makes them feel good.'

Beyond Thornton's Budgens, I hope that you'll find the financial performance of both Cotswold Fayre and Musgrave sufficiently compelling to be curious enough to try some of what we have recommended. I feel hopeful about the future and that, going forward, a sufficient number of businesses will adopt enough of the principles in this book to hit a tipping point and shift the axis of how business operates. And even if the leaders of these businesses don't read this book, it feels as if the world is naturally moving in that direction anyway.

Our legacy

Having been on this journey to becoming a heart-centred leader, I've reflected a lot on what I'd like my legacy to be. I hope I'll be able to help create many more heart-centred businesses across the globe. I see this happening through writing this book, through training business leaders to be more heartful and sitting alongside a number of those business leaders as they make their journey back to the heart. As I was writing this, a 'Legacy Reflection Aid' from a weekend course I went on a while ago fell out of an old notebook, so I filled it in. The first question asked for five reflections on my personal legacy. My answers were as follows:

1. The world needs to change to address the climate and inequality crises.

2. Having an open heart will allow businesses to be more inclusive and tackle the challenges of the climate crisis.

3. I know how to do this.

4. My sphere of influence has grown to the degree that what I say will be taken seriously by enough business leaders to make a difference.

5. This book is the platform I need to do this.

It then asked what community I wanted to strengthen with my legacy – and my reply was: the business community. Then it asked me to bring it together in a declaration of intent, and this is what I wrote:

I, Andrew Thornton, am going to strengthen my legacy to the business community by being seen as a visionary heart surgeon and publishing this book during the next three to 12 months.

Eudora has a different perspective on legacy: 'I don't care if I'm remembered after I've gone. I care about what's happening now. I try to be the best mother by being the best version of myself. I look under my rocks so that I can face the world knowing my fear, anger, pain and joy, but I don't let the rocks stop me from living to my full potential. I love supporting others to do the same. All I want for the future is for my daughter to be happy and live her life to her full potential. I gain inspiration from books like *Goodnight Stories for Rebel Girls* and *Boys Who Dare to Be Different,* where every page is devoted to a child who experienced something challenging and said no, I will no longer put up with this, and decided to do things differently. It follows their lives and shows how taking a stand impacted their world and the greater world around them. I try to keep my eyes open and make a stand when I see something that doesn't feel right or fair. That's my legacy.'

> YOUR TURN: *For the final exercise, I invite you to consider what legacy you will be leaving by undertaking the exercise above – write down five reflections on your legacy, identity the community you wish to strengthen and then bring this together into a declaration.*

I hope that you will use this book to positively change your life and the lives of those you live, work and play with. If each of you only makes one or two changes in your life as a result, then the time and effort associated with writing this book will have been worthwhile. And please do share with us any stories, experiences and questions you have – we'd love to hear from you.

In conclusion

I believe we're about to enter an unprecedented period of change in the business world. The climate crisis will dominate the agenda for at least the next decade, and whether we manage to restrict warming to 1.5 or even 2°C or it's too late and we end up with irreversible damage to the planet, I have no doubt that the heart-centred businesses are best placed to cope with this extraordinary period of turmoil. It's such a great opportunity for businesses that want to stand out from the crowd and be counted as companies that care.

With inequality, the pace of change is still too slow. On a recent visit to Selma in the Deep South of the US, it astounded me to discover that it took almost 100 years from the passing of the 15th amendment in 1870 (which granted black men the right to vote – it wasn't until 1920 that women of any colour were allowed to vote) to the Voting Rights Act, which enforced the amendment, being passed in 1965. We don't have another 100 years to straighten out the current situation with inequality. Again, this presents a great opportunity for businesses. The vast majority of the global workforce are not white males. We have demonstrated that the heart approach allows you to better engage with every single person in your business, whatever their ethnicity or background. Surely this is needed now more than ever.

Eudora notes: 'I recently met up with a friend who spent the first 30 minutes of our conversation talking about his decision on whether or not to have a Covid vaccine. It dawned on me that he didn't want to hear my opinion. When he did stop speaking, I surprised myself by saying: "You can have whatever opinion you want and make whatever choice you want because you're a single white man with no dependants and a very good job. You have the privilege of choice." The next day I turned on the radio to listen to the 75th anniversary edition of BBC Radio 4's *Woman's Hour*, where women were being invited to phone in and discuss their feelings about equality in 2021. The callers were very clear that until both parents take 100 per cent shared responsibility for the childcare and cost of their children that there won't be true equality. I thought about my own situation, bringing up my daughter for many years as a single parent, without support from my family. In 11 of the 12 years of her life I have earned more than her father and have always done the largest percentage of the childcare. How can we achieve equality between men and women if women are still doing most of the housework and childcare? We live in a world where there are more and more separated families that are also separated from the support of the extended family such as grandparents, aunts and uncles. Caroline Criado Perez has done a lot of research that shows women often don't even appear in data and their differences and circumstances aren't even considered. Without accurate data we can't even begin to discuss equality – not just gender equality but also race equality.'

In this respect, Eudora sees the work we did at Thornton's Budgens as groundbreaking: 'There is a proportionally high number of single mothers working in the store. Thornton's Budgens is a supermarket, and yet we invested in its people. The result was that the team grew closer and national and religious divisions were broken down.' She is reminded of what Sadia shared about her mother, who arrived in the UK as a single mother, not believing she had the qualifications to work in a supermarket (see her interview at the end of Chapter 1). 'Andrew took the time to train Sadia's mother and build her self-confidence. Not only has she continued to work for Thornton's Budgens for many years, but she also encouraged her children, sister and other family members to work there too. This investment in people has led to Thornton's Budgens having loyal and long-standing team members. The interviews in this book spell out clearly that this investment and trust has created more than a team – it has created a family. This has been even more relevant during the Covid pandemic, when most of the team were not able to travel home to visit their families. They knew they had the support of their Thornton's Budgens family. What I want everyone to experience is that, by facing our blocks and reconnecting with our individual purpose and what we love doing, we discover that there are so many more paths in front of us than we could have imagined.'

And finally, what about you personally? What motivates you to get up in the morning? Why do you work so hard and put so much energy into your work? What is the point and what legacy would you like to leave? I have felt so much more alive, happy and fulfilled since I embarked on my heart journey. I wish this for you too and would love you to join us. If you are touched by anything in this book, then we invite you to start a conversation with us. We'd love to get to know you and explore the heart approach.

Together, we can put the heart back into business.

Resources

Further reading

Heartful Business: *The Heart of Business: Leadership Principles for the Next Era of Capitalism,* by Hubert Joly (Harvard Business Review Press).

Being in flow: *Flow: The Classic Work on How to Achieve Happiness,* by Mihaly Csikszentmihalyi (Rider).

Happiness: *Hardwiring for Happiness: The New Brain Science of Contentment, Calm and Confidence,* by Rick Hanson (Harmony).

Shadow work: *Warrior, Magician, Lover, King: A Guide to the Male Archetypes Updated for the 21st Century,* by Rod Boothroyd (Bravo).

Inner Critic: *Make Peace with Your Mind: How Mindfulness and Compassion Can Free You from Your Inner Critic,* by Mark Coleman (New World Library).
Love Your Imposter: Be Your Best Self, Flaws and All, by Rita Clifton (Kogan Page).

Leadership: *The Fourth Bottom Line: Flourishing in an Era of Compassionate Leadership,* by Paul Hargreaves (SRA Books).

Nonviolent Communication: *Nonviolent Communication: A Language of Life*, by Marshall Rosenberg (Puddle Dancer Press).

Presence: *The Power of Now: A Guide to Spiritual Enlightenment*, by Eckhart Tolle (Yellow Kite).

Transactional analysis: *Transactional Analysis Concepts for All Trainers, Teachers and Tutors*, by Rosemary Napper and Trudi Newton (TA Resources).

Healthy living: *How Not to Die: Discover the Foods Scientifically Proven to Prevent and Reverse Disease*, by Dr Michael Greger (Pan).

Sleep: *Why We Sleep: Unlocking the Power of Sleep and Dreams*, by Matthew Walker (Scribner Book Company).

Mindfulness: *Search Inside Yourself: The Unexpected Path to Achieving Success, Happiness (and World Peace)*, by Chade-Meng Tan (HarperOne).

Source energy: *Work with Source: Realise Big Ideas, Organise for Emergence and Work Artfully with Money*, by Tom Nixon (workwithsource.com).

Finding your strengths: *StrengthsFinder 2.0: Discover your CliftonStrengths*, by Don Clifton (Gallup Press).

Being organised: *The 5 Choices: The Path to Extraordinary Productivity*, by Kory Kogon, Adam Merrill et al (Simon & Schuster).

Inspiring stories: *Good Night Stories for Rebel Girls*, by Elena Favilli, Francesca Cavallo, et al. (Simon & Schuster).

Articles

Mindfulness quieting the ego: https://psycnet.apa.org/
PsycBOOKS/toc/11771

Humour and mental health: www.helpguide.org/articles/
mental-health/laughter-is-the-best-medicine.htm

The 5 Forces communication process: www.htsorganisation.
co.uk/our-work-with-organisations

Financial impact of purpose: *Purpose and Performance: The Benefits of Following the Five Principles of a Purpose Driven Business:* www.blueprintforbusiness.org/research-purpose-and-performance/

Engagement at work: the Gallup 2013 Study, https://news.
gallup.com/poll/165269/worldwide-employees-engaged-work.
aspx

Other business resources

B Corp: www.bcorporation.net

A Plastic Planet: https://aplasticplanet.com

Personal development

Take a free top-line Human Potential Assessment:
www.heartinbusiness.org/freehpassessment

Celebration of being: www.celebrationofbeing.co.uk

COR: https://corexperience.com

The Mankind Project: https://mankindproject.org

Landmark: www.landmarkworldwide.com

Wim Hof: www.wimhofmethod.com

Miscellaneous

Be the Change cards: https://craftingconnection.com/?page_id=3426

About Heart in Business

Our purpose is to uncover the Authentic Leader in us all, trusting that profit will follow.

Our mission is to equip leaders to discover the purpose in everyone, to inspire the company to honour its reason for being, so that everyone can be in flow through unknotting and live at their full potential.

We act as advisors to business leaders and boards, we facilitate team workshops and open training programmes. We coach business leaders and help companies measure and track how much of their human potential they are accessing. We do this through our global team of specialist facilitators and coaches.

Accelerated Transformation Coaching (ATC) is our unique approach to uncovering the Authentic Leader in you and getting to the nub of what your purpose in life is. We focus on unknotting what is stopping you living a totally fulfilling life, as we believe that we are all leaders in different aspects of our lives, and that this unknotting process helps you access that leadership – it is a form of alchemy.

ATC is the thread that runs through all our work with business leaders and their teams. This proven method gets results that are rapid and long lasting, meaning your business can start to transform immediately and your people can quickly learn to develop productive and collaborative behaviours – this builds a more resilient and profitable business.

All of us at Heart in Business live and breathe the practical tools needed to be an Authentic Leader namely:

1. be your purpose
2. be in flow
3. be of integrity
4. be clear and consistent
5. be organised
6. be appreciative
7. be humble
8. be vulnerable
9. be present
10. be trusting.

It's a life's work: we fall down, learn, pick ourselves up and recommit to being the best of ourselves.

Heart in Business is a certified B.Corporation. To find out more about us, check out **www.heartinbusiness.org**.

Acknowledgements

Andrew

Having read the book, you'll now understand that gratitude and appreciation are critical skills for an Authentic Leader. I know that I couldn't have written this book without the support I've had from hundreds of people over the years. I'll do my best to appreciate those who have had the biggest impact.

To the late Declan O'Dowd, who gave me my first taste of the retail bug and taught me the basics of retail.

At University College Dublin, to Dr John Teeling, for opening my eyes that there was more to business than accountancy; and to the late Dr John Murray, for his deeply inspiring teaching on marketing.

To the small group that were the 1984 MBS Marketing Class at UCD, especially Anne Sawbridge, for pushing me on measurement; to Michael Carey, for all the introductions; and Loretta Dignam, for being a woman on purpose.

To Allan Leighton and Neil England, for modelling an engaged and inspiring leadership style during my Mars days; to Derek Woodhouse, for modelling calmness when I was far from calm; to Nigel Guthrie and Ian Saxton, for the fun they brought to my first line management role; to Paul Monk, for all his care for the next generations and all he has done with Working Options.

To Maureen Johnson, for showing me the power of positivity

and for promoting so many women to the top jobs at Research International.

To everyone who worked at SRCG during my time there and to all the clients who trusted us with their hard-earned cash – and a special thanks to my partners Neill Sherrell and Scott Annan for being part of the creation journey and for holding me to account when needed.

To Coilin Heavey, for what I learnt in the Vistage Group and that fateful cup of coffee in 2005.

To Gavin Claxton and Bryan Bardell at Musgrave and Budgens, for getting what we were about at Thornton's Budgens; to Martin Hyson for trusting me with two of his stores and to Chris Martin, for having the courage to lead Musgrave on a journey to the heart and for sharing it with you all here.

To Charles Wilson, for immediately getting the importance of the heart experiment at Thornton's Budgens and for all he did to support it in his time at Booker; and to Dave Lewis at Tesco, for being a heartful and generous leader and for all his support and encouragement with our plastic-free work.

To every single person who worked at Thornton's Budgens during the 15 years of my ownership. I'd love to name-check everyone but I'd like to highlight Neil Dugard, for managing Crouch End with all the challenges that brought; to Jim McGuire, for his skill in seeing the best in everyone and nurturing that; to Daniel Frohwein, for bringing his passion for coaching to our self-leadership journey; to Surma Begin and Kate Avgarska, for taking on the co-leadership role with such gusto and how they modelled self-leadership by learning and developing themselves at such an impressive rate; and to Parvin Nessa and Marco Amato, for being their co-deputies and always being there to support and fill in the gaps – and for how much they grew as humans.

To Shanthy Lal, who has worked alongside me for most of my entrepreneurial career. Being able to fully trust her with money gave me the freedom to do so much of what is described in this book. And for her honesty, growth and challenges, even when they were uncomfortable. And to Russell Granat, for the wise counsel provided in all financial matters.

To those in the communities of Crouch End and Belsize Park who made me so welcome. In Crouch End, to Clare Richmond, Helene Connelly, Chris Freeman, David Winskill and all the other independent retailers who cared about our community.

In Belsize Park, to Linda and Malcolm Grove, who embody what it is to be community leaders; to Alexis Rowell, for your passion; and to the team at Daunt Books – where I have sourced so much of my fiction over the years. To our very own Poet Laureate, Robert Ilson; and to Dame Janet Suzman, Tom Conti and Jim Broadbent for giving their time to help us promote our 'change the world' campaigns. And to all at Wac Arts for what you do.

To the late Lawrence Bloom, who inspired me and so many others.

To Paul Gardner, for agreeing to provide our control store.

To the whole team at A Plastic Planet, for their partnership on our plastic project, particularly Sian Sutherland for her passion, energy and make-it-happen attitude; and Frankie Gillard, for pure tenacity and keeping us on track.

To John Higginson and his team, for the amazing press coverage and the impact that had on the world of supermarket retailing; and to the team at Made Thought, for visualising the ideas in our store.

To Colm Murray, for his focus and clarity in translating our manifesto into in-store communication.

To Jonathan Webb and Richard Savage, for their support in developing our purpose at Thornton's Budgens.

To Mark Vandeneijnde and Sujith Ravindran, for what they have created with BEING at Full Potential. To Mark, for our co-creation and travels together both physically and emotionally; and Sujith, for our times together in India and the new perspective he helped me see in myself. And to all the Human Potential coaches who were so generous with their time with the Thornton's Budgens team.

To Chris Randle and Nicolas David-Ngan, for their support and encouragement in the early days of Heart in Business; and thanks to Nicolas for the initial inspiration to write this book.

To Hannah Fisher and Nathalie Vetter-Rousseau, for their support during our 'growing pains' years.

To Matt and Heather Raynor, for having the courage to be the first external business to fully say yes to the heart way of doing things. And to Paul Hargreaves and the leadership team at Cotswold Fayre, for how wholeheartedly they have embraced heartful leadership.

To Rita Clifton, for writing our foreword, for all her support for our heart work over the years, and for the deep conversations and laughter we always have when we meet.

To Justin King, for his passion for businesses that seek to be a force for good; and to Aileen Richards and Vittoria Varalli, for being passionate about female leadership and walking their talk.

To Roger Whiteside, for his honesty, the passion he always brings to his job and for the fact that I always feel energised by our conversations. To James Perry for your care and for introducing me to the B Corp movement and, with Rosie and Ed, for the creation of the amazing and heartful company, COOK.

To Azul Thome, for introducing me into the world of personal development, for the passion she applied to all aspects of her life and for how much I grew during our relationship.

To everyone at The Journey in Embercombe, for kicking off my personal development career, especially Tim 'Mac' Macartney for sharing my view on the role business has in all this; and to Jonathan Snell, for the deep insight I received during our coaching sessions.

To Tom-Fortes Mayer, for introducing me to the Celebration of Being (COB) and to Rajyo Allen, Gina Holland and Debbie Beauchamp, for years of workshops in the Isle of Wight. There's no doubt that I would not have written this book without them. To Gina, for always being there for me and Rajyo, for pushing me to do my first leadership training in the US when she saw how much I was crying out for it!

To Britta and Lee Eskey at COR in the US, for building on what I started at COB – they have taught us so much of what we use to help leaders be more heartful. And for modelling a humble 'we are flawed human beings just like you' style of teaching that I do my best to replicate. And for now giving me the chance to be part of their leadership team.

To the team at Land Celebration in Virginia, where I learnt so much about myself and how I interact with the world – thanks Suwayla, Lisa and Nate.

To everyone at the ManKind Project, for years of learning, growth and support, especially Robert Taylor and Mark Powley, and all the men in my men's group – especially Andrew Kleovoulou, for so often being there for me in my hour of need; and Chris Roche, for your authenticity and the photographs in this book.

To Noel Janis-Norton, for her wise insight into parenting and therefore into life; and to Sheryl Close, for her support through my adrenal fatigue and beyond.

To everyone at The Right Book Company, for without them this book would not exist. To Sue Richardson, for believing in this idea from day one and managing us through the process of getting these ideas down on paper; to Beverley Glick, for your amazing editing and turning what was a bit of a jumble into a compelling story; and to Paul East and Andrew Chapman for your tireless work in producing the final product.

To Ian at Dormdust Productions for producing the audio book. We certainly tested his patience with our never-ending stream of bloopers and retakes. That man must have the patience of a saint..!

To Tim Kenny, for all those years of support in retailing days, for his wisdom, friendship and that fateful pint in The Tap!

To David Taylor, for years of love, challenges and care – and that fateful breakfast question in 2005, and for being there during so many of the challenging times of my life.

To Sack Igarashi, for all those ski hills we have pounded and fun we have had – and his wisdom about focusing on what you love doing.

To my ex-wife Marian, for her support when I was giving up my life as a consultant to become a shopkeeper, and being the mother to my sons.

To my cousin Marc Thornton, for trusting me enough to follow the heart path.

To my parents, for all our moving around (especially to Holland), for their love, for the encouragement to keep learning, and for knowing they are always there for me during challenging times.

To my siblings: Jenny, for her courage and determination to have a fulfilling life and providing Mayo as a haven for me in difficult times; Rhona, for always being there to listen to me and for the Canadian part of my life; Barry, for his boundless energy, ability to stay positive and being such a present father. And to Paula, Richard and Cliodhna for being part of the glue of their families.

To my sons James and Rory. James, for his sensitivity and his care about the injustices in the world; Rory, for the determination he shows when he sets himself a goal and for the way his whole body engages when he's excited about something.

To Hanne, for all she has taught me since she came into my life seven years ago and for her wisdom and sensitivity. And for the fun the three of us have together.

And finally, to Eudora, without whom this book would not exist! For her unconditional encouragement with the heart experiment and her partnership in developing the heart way of being; for co-creating or creating so much of the material in this book; for her willingness to go on this Authentic Leadership journey with me, walking her talk; for holding me to account when I slip back into old ways; for her love, being my best friend and such a fun person to live with; for introducing Hanne into my life; and for all the adventures we've had together and will have in the future. My 50s have been my best decade so far and it's no coincidence that she has been alongside me for most of this decade.

Eudora

I would like to acknowledge my chosen family for being there for me through the dark tunnels and the joy. Thank you to Mark and Caroline Jackson, for being my heart-parents. They have held my hand through the birth of my daughter and the death of my biological parents, and been there in everyday life as well as for the important milestones.

To Sarah Pascall, for being my sister and also my friend. Her empathy and love have always remained steadfast even during the rockiest of moments. Her name will always be special and unique to me.

To Andrew Thornton, for always seeing me for who I am and loving me just as I am. To me, he is always wearing a purple velvet jacket even when he's cooking dinner!

To Hanne Clementine Pascall Vanner. I have never loved anyone more than I love her. She makes me the best version of myself, every moment of every day.

I also acknowledge my dear friends. We may not see each other every day but they are always in my heart, and they shape my decisions. I feel them on my shoulder, guiding, loving and supporting me always. Thank you for our friendship, Rebecca Prosser, Colette Sykes, Thomas Etienne and Katrin Fieberitz. I am lucky indeed.